NICHOLAS OF CUSA'S DEBATE WITH JOHN WENCK

NICHOLAS OF CUSA'S DEBATE WITH JOHN WENCK
A Translation and an Appraisal of
De Ignota Litteratura and Apologia Doctae Ignorantiae

by

JASPER HOPKINS

THE ARTHUR J. BANNING PRESS
Minneapolis

B
765
.W463
D43513
1988

THIRD EDITION

Third edition, 1988
(First edition, 1981)

Copyright © 1981 by The Arthur J. Banning Press, 1312 Foshay Tower, Minneapolis, Minnesota 55402. All rights reserved. This book may not be reproduced, in whole or in part, in any form (except by reviewers for the public press) without written permission of the Publisher.

Printed in the United States of America

Library of Congress Catalog Card Number 80-82908

ISBN 0-938060-40-6

PREFACE TO THE FIRST EDITION

This is a companion volume to my book *Nicholas of Cusa on Learned Ignorance: A Translation and an Appraisal of De Docta Ignorantia* (Minneapolis: The Arthur J. Banning Press, 1981). It presents the first English translation of John Wenck's attack on, and Nicholas's defense of, *De Docta Ignorantia*. Moreover, the appendix contains my new edition of the Latin text of Wenck's *De Ignota Litteratura*. And the introduction attempts to provide an evenhanded assessment of the occasion and the circumstances of the dispute. The extended analysis of Vincent Martin's "The Dialectical Process in the Philosophy of Nicholas of Cusa" serves two purposes: it helps furnish a backdrop against which to view Wenck's misunderstanding; and, more importantly, it exposes the shortcomings of an interpretation which, more than any other, has misdirected American philosophers in their approach to *De Docta Ignorantia*.

The translations contain numerous brackets; and these are bound to prove somewhat of an irritant. However, since they are essential for indicating words and phrases supplied by the translator, I ask the reader's forbearance, in the interest of accuracy. The goal of accuracy was also promoted by an array of persons at the University of Minnesota, all of whom willingly assisted me in proofreading various parts of the two volumes. The bibliography and the notes were double-checked by Peter Petzling; the Latin text of *De Ignota Litteratura*, by Mary Preus; portions of the Introductions and the translations, by John Augustine, Ruth Bauhahn, Stephanie Eller, Max Fritzler, Thomas Hoy, Mark Matthews, John Pepple, Judith Green, and Ruth Anne Ruud. I am grateful not only for the cheerfulness with which each rendered assistance but also for each's commitment to scholarly values. I also express indebtedness to the personnel of Wilson Library, who, with ready cooperation, obtained needed materials and made available needed facilities.

The entire project was supported by both the National Endowment for the Humanities, which awarded a stipend under its Translations Program, and the University of Minnesota, which granted an additional quarter's leave.

Jasper Hopkins
Professor of Philosophy
University of Minnesota

PREFACE TO THE THIRD EDITION

This edition revises the notes to the Latin text of *De Ignota Litteratura*. To this end, I revisited both the Stadtbibliothek in Mainz and the Stadtbibliothek in Trier. At Mainz Frau Annelen Ottermann was especially helpful in making available to me Latin manuscript 190.

A second edition of *Nicholas of Cusa on Learned Ignorance* was published in 1985.

CONTENTS

Introduction	3
On Unknown Learning (De Ignota Litteratura)	19
by John Wenck	
A Defense of Learned Ignorance (Apologia Doctae Ignorantiae)	41
by Nicholas of Cusa	
Abbreviations	69
Praenotanda	70
Cross References	72
from *Ignota Litteratura* to *Docta Ignorantia*	
from *Apologia* to *Ignota Litteratura*	
Notes	76
Appendix: Latin text of *De Ignota Litteratura*	95
Index	119

NICHOLAS OF CUSA'S DEBATE WITH JOHN WENCK

INTRODUCTION

John Wenck was born in Herrenberg, Germany during the last decade of the fourteenth century. After a period of study in Paris, where he received the title *Master of Arts* (1414), he moved to Heidelberg and began teaching at the University (1426). There he subsequently earned a license in theology (1432) and on three different occasions (1435, 1444, 1451) was elected rector. As a delegate to the tempestuous Council of Basel, he sided against the position taken by Pope Eugene IV and therefore against Nicholas of Cusa, who had broken definitively with the Conciliar Movement by 1438. Nicholas, in his *Apologia*, states that Wenck was the only teacher at the University of Heidelberg to take up "the condemned cause of the men of Basel, in which cause he presumably is tenaciously continuing. . . ."[1] Theologically, Wenck was hostile to the teachings of the Beghards and of Meister Eckhart. Philosophically, he saw himself as a defender of Thomism and its attendant Aristotelian borrowings; but he was also interested in Pseudo-Dionysius and wrote a commentary on *The Celestial Hierarchy*. Wenck's sizable scholarly output,[2] together with his prominence as teacher and rector, made his demise in 1460 a significant event in the life of the University of Heidelberg. Indeed, Gerhard Ritter, in his history of the University, refers to Wenck, not implausibly, as "the most important of the Heidelberg theologians" of that era.[3]

De Ignota Litteratura was written a few years after *De Docta Ignorantia*. Rudolf Haubst[4] dates it some time between March 26, 1442 and mid-summer of 1443. The latter date marks the death of John of Gelnhausen, Abbot of Maulbronn, to whom the work is addressed;[5] and the former date is known to be one of the times when Wenck wrote the Abbot.[6] Haubst regards the *Apologia* as written around October 9, 1449; and in doing so, he reasons as follows: At the outset the *Apologia* refers to Nicholas as "now added to the College of Cardinals," an event that occurred on December 20, 1448. Moreover, farther along in the text (19:27) the feast of St. Dionysius (October 9) is referred to as "today." Presumably, then, the work was written around October 9, 1449. Haubst is certainly right about these dates and may also be right about why Nicholas's reply came so much later than Wenck's attack: viz., that in the

Introduction

intervening time Nicholas had not seen this writing. Interestingly, Haubst came to unturn, in the Vatican Library, a reference to *De Facie Scolae Doctae Ignorantiae*, Wenck's response to Nicholas's *Apologia*. However, no manuscripts of this further work have ever been found. Haubst speculates that Wenck took pains to keep the work from Nicholas so as not to give the latter the opportunity to "malign" him once again.[7] But, of course, in the absence of any evidence, other conjectures might be equally plausible.

A printed text of *IL*[8] was first published in 1910 by Edmond Vansteenberghe.[9] But for two reasons a completely new edition is here presented: (1) Vansteenberghe's text is based upon only one of the two extant manuscripts;[10] and (2) when his text is compared with the one manuscript he used, it is seen to be riddled with errors.[11] Vansteenberghe worked too hastily and with too much disregard for critical apparatus. For example, he does not note for the reader his editorial deletion, at 27:3, of the words "*respondetur superabundat*," contained in the Mainz manuscript. True, these words do not fit meaningfully with the preceding words, for the scribe mistakenly wrote "*respondetur*" instead of "*essentialiter*," as we learn from the Trier version. Yet, as editor, Vansteenberghe should let readers know that there is a problem here. At times he misreads an abbreviation which he certainly knew—as when he puts "*destruit*" instead of "*destituit*"(36:9) or puts "*amplius*" instead of "*apostolus*" (39:18). At other times he misreads an abbreviation which he most likely did not know—as when he puts "*summarum*" instead of "*Sententiarum*" (27:19) or puts "*Physicorum*" instead of "*Perihermeniarum*" (35:20). Other of his errors are simple errors of proofreading at the time of printing.

In his editor's introduction Vansteenberghe attributes to *IL* "only a minimal importance" (p. 3). And this evaluation explains, perhaps, the casualness and the carelessness with which he worked.[12] As a result of his edition, seven decades of students have come to regard Wenck's competency in Latin as extraordinarily low. To be sure, it is not extraordinarily high; indeed, it is not high at all. But it is much better than Vansteenberghe's edition would ever lead anyone to believe. By comparison, when Wenck writes in German, his literary style is vastly improved. For example, Georg Steer, the editor of Wenck's *Büchlein von der Seele*, can rightly point to the *Büchlein's "klare Gliederung,"* its *"geschmeidige Sprache,"* and its *"Vielzahl ursprünglicher Bilder und treffender Vergleiche."*[13]

The meaning of the title which Wenck gives to his work is not immediately clear. One's first impression is that it probably means "on ignorant learning"—thus making a nice contrast with "on learned ignorance." But in explaining the title he does not interpret it in such way as to be calling Nicholas's work the product of ignorance. The title of Nicholas's book, he explains, indicates the two boundaries of any inquiry: viz., setting out from *what is known* and moving inferentially to *what is unknown*. Wenck keeps these two boundaries in his own title: *"De Ignota Litteratura"*: *"On Unknown Learning"*—a title suggested by the words of Isaiah 29:11–12 and of Psalms 70:15–16 (71:15–16). The former verses speak of a sealed book's being given to "one who does not know letters"; and in the latter verses David declares that he does "not know learning" but nonetheless "will enter into the powers of the Lord." But the unknown learning to which Wenck refers is that which characterized the Apostle Paul: "For even the Teacher of the Gentiles—who judged himself to know nothing among the Corinthians except Jesus Christ and Him crucified—did not deny other knowledge, in which he abounded. Instead, he offered the Corinthians the unknown learning of the sealed book, which is Christ Jesus."[14] As Paul offered unknown learning to the haughty Corinthians, so Wenck offers to Nicholas, also regarded as swollen with pride, a learning—a Christ—that Nicholas is presumed not yet to know. Like Paul, Wenck wants to glory in Jesus Christ and in Him only. He regards *DI* as worldly erudition which has a semblance of godliness but which leads away from the truth of the Gospel.[15] Nicholas is said to lack the eyesalve spoken of in Revelation 3:17–18. For he does not understand Christ's humanity, "which is the salve of our eyes for seeing the glory of God. . . ."[16] Because Nicholas does not understand the doctrine of Christ, he also does not understand the doctrine of God or the truth about God's relationship to the world. In his pride and lack of leisure, alleges Wenck, Nicholas has disobeyed the Psalmist's command "Be still and see that I am God."[17] Thus, he has become vain in his thoughts; and amid his *curiositas et vanitas*[18] he resorts to stratagems such as the doctrine that in God *contradictoria coincidunt*.[19] Wenck, for his part, prefers to be guided foremostly by Scripture and to be aligned with the Psalmist, who, in order to enter into the light of the Lord, had no need of such learning as Nicholas's—a learning which is darkness.

What were Wenck's motives in writing *IL* and in hurling the foregoing charges? Were the charges primarily the distorted products of emotional hostility resulting from the Council of Basel?[20] Vansteenberghe does not care to deny the existence of some such prejudice. But he goes on to add: "Between the author of *De Docta Ignorantia* and his adversary there is more than a deplorable personal quarrel: there is a discussion which is truly and purely philosophical and theological."[21] And Gerhard Ritter judges that Wenck's pious zeal for orthodoxy would be sufficient by itself to explain his attack, even though the attack might also have something to do with the events of the Council of Basel.[22] Rudolf Haubst, who deals at length with the issue of Wenck's motivation, cites a combination of three factors: First, there was indeed the element of Wenck's having taken up, and Nicholas's having turned

Introduction

aside from, "the condemned cause of the men of Basel."[23] According to Haubst, this political difference was "the hidden motive without which Wenck would not have written his invective against *De Docta Ignorantia* in the way he did—and perhaps would not have written it at all."[24] Secondly, Wenck was out to dispose of all heretics, among whom he counted Nicholas; for he saw him as associated with the heresy of the Beghards. Finally, he likewise was defending the scientific nature of philosophy and theology against what he regarded as Nicholas's repudiation of Aristotelian logic and of the Thomistic doctrine of *analogia entis*. Unlike Ritter, Haubst does not think that Wenck's zeal for orthodoxy can by itself account for the vehement character of *IL*; but unlike Nicholas himself Haubst seems not to regard Wenck as primarily a *falsarius*, a falsifier,[25] intent mainly on blackening Nicholas's reputation by truncation and perverse interpretation.[26]

While agreeing with Haubst's three points insofar as they are sketched above, students of the controversy will want to explore more fully the causes of Wenck's misunderstanding of *DI*—a misunderstanding which led him to deem *DI* heretical and unscientific. It will become apparent that Wenck's misconstruals are honest mistakes and not, as Nicholas supposed, deliberate and malevolent distortions. Of course, a determined critic of Wenck can always insist on attributing each of the mistaken citations of *DI* to evil motives—if the critic is willing to pay the hermeneutical price, which in this case will be quite high. For it is highly implausible to suppose that Wenck—a respected professor at Heidelberg and already a former rector—would deliberately and openly have misquoted a work which was in wide enough circulation to be available to the audience for whom he was writing. Only someone very foolish, someone blinded by rage, someone unscrupulous, or all three, would have proceeded in such a way. But from the respect paid to Wenck by the University community which thrice elected him rector, and from the fact that his treatise against Nicholas is coherent, well organized, and not uncontrolled in tone,[27] we may reliably eliminate each of these alternatives.

The misreadings which incensed Wenck and induced him to view Nicholas as a heretic are the result of a combination of factors other than malice. In particular, there seem to be three causes of misunderstanding: (1) Nicholas's use of vague and imprecise expressions whose meanings are never explicitly expounded, (2) Wenck's hasty and superficial reading of *DI*, and (3) the likelihood of scribal errors in the manuscript upon which Wenck based his criticisms.

1. We have already seen, in *Nicholas of Cusa on Learned Ignorance*, a number of examples of Nicholas's misleading terminology: his use of the word "emanation" with regard to creation; his talk about the believer's being absorbed into Christ and being resurrected as Christ; his statement that Christ *is*

Introduction

each believer; his penchant for the language-of-enfoldedness, which creates the impression that as enfolded in God finite things retain their finitude and their identities; the unclarity about what position he is endorsing when he discusses the topic of the world-soul; and his use of the word "actually" in the sentence "An infinite line is actually and infinitely all that which is in the possibility of a finite line." Moreover, we have been puzzled by other statements which he at times only halfway explains, at times explains in terms of examples which themselves need elucidation. For instance, the significations of the key noun "contraction" and the key verb "to contract" are never adequately unpacked. Likewise, the verb "to coincide" is used misleadingly in the sentence which states that in Jesus "the human things coincide with the divine things." Nor from an initial reading is it clear in what sense God is present in all things through the mediation of the universe. Furthermore, *ratio* sometimes seems to be distinguished from *intellectus* and sometimes not—leaving the reader confused. Some of the reasoning—e.g., the passage in I, 4 about the Maximum coinciding with the Minimum—is so obviously specious that it can only irritate a sensible reader. Some claims are even nonsensical: "The plurality of things arises from the fact that God is present in nothing." As if these woes were not bad enough, Nicholas sometimes adds to them—as at places in I, 18—by switching back and forth between an illustration and the illustrated, without giving any clear signal to the reader that a transition is being made. Little wonder that Wenck should have become both exasperated and confused!

There is no better way to exonerate Wenck than to show how twentieth-century interpreters, whom surely no one could ever accuse of personal animosity, have misinterpreted *DI* at least as badly as did Wenck. Although the number of such interpreters is legion, we may focus, for pedagogical reasons, on Vincent Martin's "The Dialectical Process in the Philosophy of Nicholas of Cusa" as a paradigm case of contemporary misconstrual.[28]

a. Martin construes the doctrine of *coincidentia oppositorum* along the following lines:

> By contending that in the maximum, diversity is identity, Cusa must mean that, in the maximum, the past *qua* past is distinct from the future; but, since diversity is identity, the past, although properly distinct from the future, is at the same time not properly distinct from the future. He must mean that, in the eternity of God, those things which are formally predicated of[29] creatures—namely, past, present and future—are properly divine because they are at the maximum; and, being divine, they are properly identified one with the other. Yet again, since they are the maximum of formalities said of the creatures, they are properly created and therefore distinct one from the other. In identity they are distinct; in distinction, identical—for in the maximum, diversity is identity.[30]

But this construal is deviant. For Nicholas never asserts, and nowhere implies, that in the Maximum the past qua past is distinct from the future. In the passage

Introduction

which Martin has in mind (viz., *DI* I, 21) Nicholas states: "In the Maximum all difference is identity. Hence, since the Maximum's power is most one, its power is also most powerful and most infinite. The Maximum's most one duration is so great that in its duration the past is not other than the future, and the future is not other than the present; rather, they are the most one duration, or eternity, without beginning and end." Here Nicholas is clear about the fact that in the Maximum past, present, and future coincide and are one eternity. Curiously, Martin stops his Latin quotation (on his p. 224) before the clause that begins with the word "*sed*," which corresponds to the English word "rather" in the foregoing sentence. Why did Martin omit so crucial a clause? Would not Nicholas call him just as much a *truncator* as Wenck? Similarly, Martin fails to view this passage, and to interpret the doctrine of *coincidentia*, in the light of I, 24 (77:1–7): "Who could understand the infinite Oneness which infinitely precedes all opposition?—where all things are incompositely enfolded in simplicity of Oneness, where there is neither anything which is other nor anything which is different, where a man does not differ from a lion, and the sky does not differ from the earth. Nevertheless, in the Maximum they are most truly the Maximum, [though] not in accordance with their finitude; rather, [they are] Maximum Oneness in an enfolded way." Although the doctrine of *coincidentia* and the doctrine of *complicatio* (enfoldedness) are in some respects different, they are alike in teaching that whatever is enfolded in God, or whatever coincides in God, is not in God qua its finite self.[31] Would not Nicholas accuse Martin, as he accused Wenck, of violating the following precept?: "Whoever examines the mind of someone writing on some point ought to read carefully all his writings and ought to resolve [his statements on this point] into one consistent meaning."[32]

Martin also asserts, on the basis of Nicholas's conception of Divinity as the *coincidentia oppositorum*, that "God is the mere resolution of what is impossible in creation."[33] But this claim is also wrong, for Nicholas teaches that God's power is not exhausted in this present creation and that given any creature whatsoever, God can create one that is more perfect.[34] It follows that God is much more than the "mere resolution of what is impossible in creation." For He is also the actuality of all the *possible* but uncreated things.[35]

Martin also teaches that, for Nicholas, God is conceived as "the ultimate limit towards which all things converge," that God's otherness is "enclosed and measured by the creatures converging towards it."[36] Later he offers an example to help explain Cusa's point. Surprisingly, it is not one of Nicholas's many examples but one of Martin's own: "We may compare the maximum to the number 2, say, as the limit of the series 1, 1 + 1/2, 1 + 1/2 + 1/4 . . . For 2 is, as it were, the unattainable maximum of the increasing sums of the series. The series remains open to ever greater sums. Each new sum differs less from

Introduction

the maximum, but none will ever be equal to it. Note, too, that at the same time the increasing sums converge toward a minimum, since any sum of the series differs by less from the preceding one, and by more from the next. Hence, both the maximum and the minimum of the series lie beyond the series, where they coincide. This again is in keeping with Cusa's paradoxical description of God as both 'maximum' and 'minimum.' "[37] But here again Martin is completely wrong: Nicholas does not maintain that creatures *converge* towards God or that God and His otherness are *measured* by creatures converging toward Him. In fact, Nicholas plainly states that "what is contracted [falls short] of what is absolute—the two being infinitely different";[38] and, according to II, 9, "God alone is absolute; all other things are contracted."[39] In Martin's number series the series of sums falls only infinitesimally short of 2; but Nicholas denies that the creation falls only infinitesimally short of the Creator. Though he calls each thing a created god and a god manqué, it is obvious that this is a manner of speaking intended to reinforce the notion that each created thing qua created thing is as perfect as *it* can be. Neither an angel nor the whole of creation is only infinitesimally short of being God Himself. This is why Nicholas can affirm that created things have even less being than an accident,[40] that they are but a reflection of God. Moreover, between the Creator and the creation there is no comparative relation; therefore, the Creator cannot be either measured by creatures or enclosed by them. Nicholas teaches that God is as different from the creation as an infinite line is different from a finite line. He does not teach that God is as different from the creation as a finite number (e.g., the number 2) is different from another finite number, or from a series of finite numbers. Martin has entirely missed the central point of *DI*—missed it just as widely as did Wenck. (Moreover, Martin is not averse to name-calling and so does not hesitate to label Nicholas's view insidious.)[41] Would not Nicholas term Martin a user of perverse interpretation, just as he did Wenck?[42]

b. Having made all of the preceding exegetical errors, Martin now has no hope of salvaging his interpretation, which is globally wrong. Indeed, he sinks deeper and deeper into his exegetical quagmire. For he interprets *DI* II, 8 as affirming that "God is the material cause from which all the creatures proceed."[43] Ever more confused, Martin writes: "Cusa has already conceived God as the greatest possible creature by envisaging Him as the maximum of the creatures. Hence, if the material principle from which all creatures come were in the created order, there would be a real potency on the part of the creatures to become God. This, on the other hand, he could never admit. Once he has made the mistake of attributing a material principle to every creature, Cusa is forced to maintain that this material principle can only be something divine."[44]

But this whole passage is mistaken. For one thing, Nicholas does not conceive of God as the greatest possible creature, for he does not conceive of

Introduction

Him as at all a creature except insofar as the Son of God became incarnate. (But Martin is not discussing Nicholas's views on incarnation but his views on creation.) And one wonders whether it is any worse for Wenck to have attributed to Nicholas the view that all things coincide with God than it is for Martin to attribute to him the view that God is the greatest possible creature. But for another thing, *DI* II, 8 does not contain the doctrine that God is the material cause from which all creatures proceed. God is said to be Absolute Possibility; but Absolute Possibility qua God is not matter, according to Nicholas. Martin makes the same kind of mistake that Wenck made vis-à-vis Nicholas's discussion of the world-soul in II, 9: viz., he attributes to Nicholas a view which Nicholas examines but does not endorse. Thus, Wenck in the first corollary of thesis eight ascribes to Nicholas the doctrine that "the world-soul is the unfolding of the Divine Mind." Yet, with these words Nicholas is merely expounding the views of certain Platonists, not putting forth his own theory. Similarly, at the beginning of II, 8 Nicholas sets forth the opinions of "the ancients" that from nothing nothing is made; "and so, they maintained that there is a certain absolute possibility of being all things and that it is eternal. . . . Nevertheless, they did not maintain that absolute possibility is coeternal with God, since it is from God." He goes on to present the views of various Platonists and of various Peripatetics—and then his own. Because the chapter begins with the ancients' identifying absolute possibility with matter, Martin wrongly concludes that when Nicholas presents his own views, he is still using *"possibilitas absoluta"* to signify matter! However, Nicholas's point is that "in God absolute possibility is God, but it is not possible outside Him."[45] That is, in God absolute possibility is not matter but is God Himself. Now, God Himself is Being itself. So He is beyond the distinction between the material and the immaterial; therefore, He cannot be either material or a material cause. Moreover, possibility as it exists outside of God, is always contracted through actuality;[46] only possibility contracted in a certain way is matter.[47] Martin's reading of *DI* is no more careful than was Wenck's.[48]

c. Martin now draws a consequence consistent with his mistaken interpretation that God is "the maximum of the creatures": viz., the consequence that, for Nicholas, "God and the creature have the same proper nature."[49] This inference is all the more astounding since this very statement is never found in Cusa's writings and since the *Apologia* indicates that creatures have their own respective being and form;[50] likewise, *DI* III, 1 indicates that an individual thing within a species "contracts, in its own degree, the one nature of its own species."[51] But instead of letting these and other texts condemn his theory, Martin uses his theory to condemn these texts: "It is true that, in a certain sense, Cusa does speak of different essences and different natures. He does admit that the contracted essence of the sun is different from the contracted essence of the

Introduction

moon. But these admissions, as Cusa understands them, only mean this: the essence of moon and sun are really only one essence, the absolute essence of God; but because of the subjects involved, *per accidens* and *contingenter* they are unity in plurality, unity in otherness, i.e., one essence in two subjects. But the otherness, which arises from the subjects involved, is outside the order of essence. Therefore, if we regard the essence of the sun and the moon in themselves, i.e., apart from all subjects, we are really faced with the absolute unity of the divine essence."[52] But Martin's interpretive inference is erroneous; for Nicholas does not hold the view that the essence of moon and sun are really the absolute essence of God.[53] Rather, he teaches that the Absolute Essence is the Essence of essences in the sense already explained in the Introduction of *Nicholas of Cusa on Learned Ignorance*. Martin notices that in II, 4 Nicholas uses the expression "*quiditas solis absoluta*" and "*quiditas absoluta lunae*" and that he identifies Absolute Quiddity with God. Martin then concludes that the essence of the sun (or of the moon) is, apart from all subjects, the Divine Essence. But there is something strange about this conclusion. For in II, 4 the sun's essence (*quiditas*) is said to be a contracted essence; and God is said to be uncontracted (i.e., absolute) Essence. Therefore, as implied by II, 4: insofar as it makes sense to talk about the sun or its essence it does not make sense to talk about it as uncontracted; and insofar as there is discourse about uncontracted Essence, it is not discourse about the sun's essence. So Martin's attempt to talk about the essence of the sun apart from all subjects (i.e., as uncontracted) is unintelligible, given Nicholas's terminology. Even Nicholas's expression "*quiditas solis absoluta*" does not mean "the sun's Absolute Quiddity," for the sun qua sun has no Absolute Quiddity but has only a contracted quiddity, which gives it its being as *sun*. Rather, "*quiditas solis absoluta*" ("Absolute Quiddity of the sun") is a *modus loquendi* that has reference to God, who is the Absolute Quiddity of all things, and therefore also of the sun. Both in *DI* I and the *Apologia* Nicholas explains that God is the Absolute Quiddity of all things in that He is the Quiddity of all (contracted) quiddities—just as He is the Absolute Being of all things in that He is the Being of all beings. There is no doubt that Nicholas himself should have been more circumspect in his use of such easily misinterpretable locutions. But for one reason or another he could not imagine that his readers would be so prone to misapprehension. Even at the time of writing the *Apologia*, he does not concede that there is anything amiss in his terminology, but instead pushes all the blame onto Wenck: "That man understands nothing at all. For God is the Quiddity of all quiddities and is the Absolute Quiddity of all things—even as He is the Absolute Being of beings and the Absolute Life of living things. (The church expresses this in prayer: 'God, Life of living things,' . . . and so on.) To say this is not to confound or to destroy the quiddities of things but to

Introduction

establish them, as wise men recognize."[54] Though Nicholas must share some of the blame for his readers' woes, the fact remains that someone like Martin would not so readily have misunderstood these expressions had he not previously misunderstood so much else that was much clearer.[55]

d. Martin now moves to his finale, which stops just short of accusing Nicholas of pantheism: "Creatures, then, as conceived by Cusa, are really divinity in privation. If the difference between God and the creature is merely privative, there can be no positive difference between 'what God is' and 'what the creature is'; God and the creature must be identical as to their positive being. Because of the privation, the creature cannot be called divine, for it does not have the total perfection of divinity; but the perfection which it does possess must be divinity."[56] On p. 257 Martin adds: "According to this conception, God must be considered as having two states of being: one, with privation; the other, without privation. God without privation is God as He is in Himself; God with privation is God as He is in the creatures. But in either state the actuality, the positive being, is exactly the same. The only difference would be that one state would have relatively more positive being than the other." In elaborating this interpretation Martin writes: "A creature is not one being and God another being, as though two beings were involved. The being of a creature is not something other than the divine being; rather, the being of a creature is intrinsically constituted by the divine being. Its intrinsic being (its *ab esse*) is the divinity within it. It has absolute necessity inasmuch as its positive content, i.e., that by which (*a qua*) it is constituted, is the divine being. It also has the note of contingency owing to the privation without which it would not be a creature (*sine qua non est*)."[57]

Once again, Martin has failed to take seriously the statements in *DI* and the *Apologia* to the effect that creatures have their own respective forms and their own respective being. Martin thinks that, for Nicholas, God differs from His creation in that He is total perfection, whereas the creation possesses only incomplete divine perfection. Yet, what Nicholas teaches is something quite different: viz., that the respective contracted perfections and contracted natures of creatures bear no comparative relation to Divine Perfection, which is infinite and uncontracted. For—to repeat a theme passage—"what is contracted [falls short] of what is absolute—the two being infinitely different,"[58] so that there can be no *proportio*. Martin's depiction of God as having two states of being—one without privation and one with privation—seriously misrepresents Nicholas's doctrines. According to Martin, the difference between these two states is that "one state would have relatively more positive being than the other." But Nicholas's whole point in calling God *Absolute* and *Being itself* is to deny that God's being is subject to such relativity. Similarly, when Martin urges that "a creature is not one being and God another being, as though two

Introduction

beings were involved," he misapprehends Nicholas's point and thus goes on to allege that "the being of a creature is not something other than the divine being." He should rather say that, for Nicholas, a creature is not one being and God another in the same domain of comparison; for God is not *a* being but is undifferentiated Being itself. Precisely because He is undifferentiated Being He cannot be the contracted being of any creature—i.e., cannot be any creature's contracted being. Rather, He is the Cause of that creature's being. Though the creature's being is contingent (i.e., dependent) being, it is nonetheless *that* creature's contingent being. True, Nicholas calls created being only a reflection; and he denies that it is a reflection *received positively* in some other thing.[59] But it does not follow that a created thing has no positive being, has no being of its own. What follows is that a created thing's positive being derives, in an ultimate sense, wholly from God because it was created *ex nihilo* and did not emanate forth from God into some modifying receptacle that is eternally other than God, as the Platonists taught.

Martin's main purpose in writing his lengthy article was to point out the "devaluation of Divinity in the philosophy which Cusa advances under the guise of a deep and mystical understanding of His transcendence."[60] Like Wenck, Martin is out to expose the deceptiveness of Nicholas's philosophy, which does the reverse of what it pretends to. But in executing his task, Martin misunderstands the program of learned ignorance as extensively as did Wenck. Since Martin's misunderstanding does not result from evil motives or from lack of intellectual giftedness, it instructs us to beware of imputing Wenck's misunderstanding to malevolence stemming from the Council of Basel. Nicholas's own unclarity of expression, more than Wenck's impurity of motive, engendered Wenck's incomprehension.

2. A further cause of Wenck's inapprehension was his hasty and superficial reading of *DI*. Signs of his cursory reading appear everywhere. We have already seen the example of his ascribing to Nicholas himself a view which Nicholas attributes to the Platonists: viz., the view that the world-soul is the unfolding of the Divine Mind.[61] Another sign of superficial reading occurs in Wenck's fourth thesis, where *DI* is quoted as asserting that "the likeness of the original is the same—in oneness of nature—as the original." This citation altogether misses Nicholas's point that "except for the Maximal Image (which is, in oneness of nature, the very thing which its Exemplar is) no image is so similar or equal to its exemplar that it cannot be infinitely more similar and equal."[62] Wenck fails to realize that when Nicholas speaks of the likeness of the original as one in nature with the original, he is referring to the Son of God, whom Scripture (Col. 1:15) calls the Image of the Father; he is not referring to the universe. Reading hastily, Wenck did not detect the switch in reference from the one maximum (viz., the universe) to the other maximum (viz., the

Introduction

Maximal Image). Or again, in the first corollary of the sixth thesis, Wenck's extract from *DI* is garbled. For it construes Nicholas's statement about a maximum triangle as if it were a statement about the unqualifiedly Maximum— thereby confusing Nicholas's mathematical example with what the example is supposed to illustrate about the unqualifiedly Maximum.

In general, Wenck makes no attempt to cite *DI* exactly: he abridges, combines, reemphasizes, rephrases. There is nothing wrong, in principle, with his proceeding in this way if he chooses to. But in so proceeding he sometimes makes mistakes which could have been avoided by a careful reading. We know from the *explicit* in the Trier manuscript of *IL* that Wenck considered his own treatise to be a mere sketch;[63] and we know from the foregoing examples that he had read *DI* only superficially. If we were to speculate about why he did not take more pains in critiquing *DI*, we might well come to believe that he did not deem *DI* to be worth more time. He thought it so flagrantly heretical that he need only point out, in a spotty way, some of its dangerous deviations from the truth.

3. Wenck seems to have been working with a manuscript which in places was defective. For instance, the second corollary of thesis four attributes the following view to *DI*: "Our ignorance will teach [us], incomprehensibly, how we are supposed to think more correctly and truly about the Most High as we grope by means of a symbolism." But *DI* I, 12 (33:16) has: "Our ignorance will be taught incomprehensibly. . . ." Wenck attacks by asking, polemically, how *ignorance* can teach anything at all. In mistaking Nicholas's passive verb "*docebitur*" for the active verb "*docebit*," Wenck may, of course, simply have misread the abbreviation. But since he was not so bad a Latinist as Vansteenberghe has led us to believe, it seems not unreasonable to ascribe the mistake to the manuscript rather than to Wenck himself. Another likely candidate for a manuscript problem occurs in the same corollary—in the sentence succeeding the one about our ignorance teaching us: "This is evident from the fact that ignorance is altogether independent of all figure and likewise transcends the forms of finite and relational things." Wenck protests that ignorance never had a form from which to be freed. But a comparison with the text of *DI* I, 12 (33:13–15) discloses that Nicholas is making a completely different point; and the difference between the two texts is too gross to be plausibly accounted for by the hypothesis that Wenck simply misread an accurate version thereof. A final example of a manuscript problem may be found in the second corollary of the first thesis, where *IL* has the word "unfolding" ("*explicatio*"), even though the text of *DI*, in all the manuscripts used by Hoffmann and Klibansky, has "enfolding" ("*complicatio*").

We are now in a position to appreciate the fact that the debate between Wenck and Nicholas is no simple affair of emotion, no "*misérable querelle*

Introduction

personnelle,'' as Vansteenberghe rightly points out. Of course, like anyone, Wenck had mixed motives, some of which must have been personal. But it is difficult to believe that these alone moved him to pen *IL*. He was not out to "get even with Nicholas" by deliberately distorting his statements. Yet, the earlier strife at Basel was probably a necessary condition of his bothering to write his treatise, though it would not have been a sufficient condition. If he could show that Nicholas really did hold heretical views, his doing so would serve to vindicate his own opinions regarding pope and council—vindicate them at least insofar as they discredited Nicholas by showing that he was not a clearheaded thinker, something Wenck honestly believed. The psychological assessment of the motivation of distant historical figures—the records of whose lives are filled with gaps—is bound to be inconclusive. Where the data are incomplete, an historian's appraisals can only be tentative. The historical account developed in the preceding pages has agreed with Haubst regarding the factors that constitute the jointly sufficient set of conditions that motivated Wenck's treatise. But it has gone on to explore the causes of Wenck's having come to regard *DI* as heretical and unscientific. And it has suggested that Nicholas himself, by his manner of presentation, must bear much of the responsibility for having engendered Wenck's misapprehension.

Contemporary scholarship has succeeded in making Wenck look worse than his available record warrants. Scholars have taken too seriously Nicholas's accusations of falsification, truncation, mendacity, and perverse interpretation—tending to accept these appraisals instead of modulating Nicholas's own vilification of Wenck and instead of calling attention to Nicholas's own blindness regarding the misleading aspects of many of his own expressions. Moreover, Vansteenberghe's edition of *IL* has too long prevailed, implanting the impression that Wenck was almost illiterate in Latin. At the same time, scholars have minimized the admirable features of organization which characterize *IL*: its orchestration around the text of Psalms 45:11 (46:10), which it takes as its theme; its subtle eliciting of its title from Scripture; its clear division into theses and corollaries—and the further division of each of these into an *assertio* and a *probatio*. Without doubt, Wenck was handicapped by his lack of facility with Latin—making it difficult for historians to determine which of the inadequacies in his work were due to linguistic limitations and which of them were due to limitations of philosophical ability. But in coming to some decision, historians need to remember that Nicholas too was guilty of misrepresentation,[64] unintentional though it be, and that the text of *DI* is filled with sentences rendered misreadable by virtue of inelegant or faulty style.

In dealing with the debate between Wenck and his opponent, we have hitherto taken for granted that this opponent was Nicholas of Cusa—i.e., that Nicholas was the author of the *Apologia*. This assumption has sometimes been

Introduction

challenged on the grounds that (1) the ostensible author is the narrator, who presents himself as a disciple of Nicholas's, and that (2) the quality of the Latin in the *Apologia* is significantly inferior to that found in the works which are unquestionably Cusa's. However, Raymond Klibansky, in his editor's introduction to the Heidelberg Academy edition of the text, cites the two main reasons why there can be no doubt about the authorship: (1) the *Apologia* is included in Codex Cusanus 218, one of the two volumes into which Nicholas collected his works; (2) Nicholas indicated in the margin at the end of the copy of the *Apologia* in Codex 218 that he had read the transcription and approved of it.[65] As for the two considerations that initially occasioned doubt: The quality of the Latin is not inferior to that of the other works contained in Cusanus 218 and 219; it only *appeared* inferior to those who judged it by the version printed in the Paris edition of 1514, which, though generally of high quality, contained a disproportionate number of editorial mistakes vis-à-vis the *Apologia*. And, secondly, though the narrator claims to be only a disciple of Nicholas's, this claim is easily construable—all things considered—as a literary device.

We have yet to reckon with a central hermeneutical problem: viz., to what extent it is legitimate to interpret *DI* through the perspective given in the *Apologia*, written over nine years later. Had not Nicholas's position undergone such a variety of developments that Nicholas himself would in subtle ways invariably have read these back into *DI* when defending it against reproach? Only a close comparison of both works will provide an answer to this question, which dare not be begged by invoking *a priori* principles about "what must be the case" in cases like this.

We see immediately that changes have indeed occurred. For example, the distinction between *ratio* and *intellectus* has become explicit in the *Apologia*, though it was not present at all in *DI* I and was not fully explicit even in *DI* III. (But it *was* explicitly present as early as *De Coniecturis*.) Or again, in *Apologia* 8:14–16 Nicholas writes: "No one was ever so foolish as to maintain that God, who forms all things, is anything other than that than which a greater cannot be conceived." But this description of God is nowhere present in *DI*. Nor is it entailed by the description of the Maximum as "all that which can be" or as "that than which there cannot be anything greater." For the language of conceivability and the language of possibility are not fully interchangeable. (E.g., God is greater than is conceivable by us but not greater than is possible.) Or again, in *Apologia* 15:14–15 God is said to be *beyond* the coincidence of contradictories;[66] but no comparable expression occurs in *DI*.

Josef Koch argues that Nicholas's position changed extensively between the completion of *DI* and the commencement of *De Coniecturis*. Koch is impressed by the fact that many of the topics which *DI* says will elsewhere be discussed never make their way into *De Coniecturis*—e.g., the problem of universals.

Introduction

Koch sees in this fact a sign that Nicholas's thought underwent a metamorphosis. His impression is reinforced by the strikingly different character of *DI* and *De Coniecturis*. Koch comes to portray this difference as a difference between two metaphysics: characteristic of *DI* is a *Seinsmetaphysik*; characteristic of *De Coniecturis*, an *Einheitsmetaphysik*. To the former metaphysic, but not to the latter, allegedly belong "the analogy of being, the distinction of degrees of being, the doctrine that all beings are composed of essence and act of being, and [the doctrine] that the essence of all material objects consists of form and matter. Thereto belongs also the acceptance of the principle of contradiction as an ontological law . . . . "[67] If Koch is correct, then there is good reason to expect that the *Apologia* would turn out to be significantly different from *DI*. For example, Wenck criticized Nicholas for having rejected, at the time of writing *DI*, the principle of *proportio*, or *analogia*.[68] Now, if Nicholas held to the doctrine of *analogia entis* in *DI*, as Koch asserts, but abandoned it afterwards, then we would expect this fact to be reflected in his response to Wenck. But his reply[69] neither corrects Wenck by declaring that the doctrine of analogy *is* present in *DI* nor intimates any subsequent change of position.

The further intricacies of this hermeneutical issue need not detain us here. Readers of the *Apologia*, being now apprised of a possible difficulty, may examine the document with more leisure than is available in the present Introduction. As they proceed to do so, however, they may well begin to have doubts about there ever having occurred a radical transition from *Seins-* to *Einheitsmetaphysik*.

The *Apologia* ought to be seen as more than a mere accessory to *DI*. For though it *is* an appendage, it is an indispensable one. The clarification of the relationship between Form and forms, the reaffirmation of the doctrine of *nulla proportio infiniti ad finitum*, the explicit assignment of a role to the principle of noncontradiction, the reiteration of the notion of *complicatio*, the clear exposition of the role of learned ignorance, the direct rejection of pantheism—all provide a much-needed finale to *DI*. We may lament the fact that Nicholas's patience in writing the *Apologia* did not last long enough for him to restate and reillustrate the major themes of his Christology. He seems never to have doubted their perfect clarity to intelligent men of good will. If the truth be known, it was Nicholas himself who regarded the *Apologia* as a mere accessory—something which he should not have had to write at all, something which, had it not been for Wenck, would have been altogether superfluous. But Wenck—whom he called arrogant, ignorant, and mad—had forced this task upon him. And so, he furnished the necessary partial clarification—being "in a hurry to nullify what was written in *Unknown Learning*."[70]

In the midst of the *Apologia* Nicholas praises Meister Eckhart's genius and ardor.[71] At the same time, he expresses regret that the common people were unable to appreciate Eckhart's subtle points. In a way, Nicholas's own failure to be appreciated by Wenck and others[72] resembles the failure of Eckhart. For like Eckhart he insisted on making statements which he construed in a special sense but which incautious readers would be prone to construe in a less restricted way. To say "God is all things"[73] or "God is the Being of things"[74] or "Every created thing is, as it were, . . . a created god"[75] was destined to provoke outcries from the orthodox, in the absence of explicit qualifications placed upon these statements. Nicholas's qualifications were not fully explicit. The ensuing tragedy consists both in the fact that his teachings have so often been so globally misconstrued and in the fact that he partly brought this fate upon himself. Though he clung to the traditional theological dogmas, he wanted to restate them with the help of mathematical symbolism and on the basis of his metaphysic of contraction. This desire led him to envelop the dogmas in a language too uncustomary for his audience. Many of his theological contemporaries who still savored the old wine did not recognize its vintage when it was served to them from new bottles. Something indeed had changed—not the dogmas themselves but their philosophical underpinnings. The newness of the metaphysic of contraction still contained something of the oldness of the Thomistic-Aristotelian distinctions between substance and accident, essence and existence, form and matter, potentiality and actuality; but the creation, qua derived being, was said not to be understandable since the Being from which it derives is not understandable.[76]

In last analysis, then, *DI* is seen to be a blend of the mathematical, the metaphysical, and the mystical. It is neither a thoroughgoing syncretism, nor a thoroughgoing metamorphosis, of the past. Yet, it is one of a cluster of fifteenth-century works that, collectively, mark an intellectual turning point: the transition from Middle Ages to Renaissance. The subsequent works of the man from Cusa do not abandon the method of learned ignorance; and yet, they do not attain the grandeur and luster of the treatise of 1440. For none of them are as sweeping in scope, as coherent in conceptualization, as elegant in organization. In spite of its monumental qualities, *DI* was doomed to provoke criticism and misunderstanding. For some of its bold and imprecise expressions made it seem theologically heretical and philosophically unsophisticated. Historically speaking, then, the appearance of John Wenck's *De Ignota Litteratura* cannot be judged as startling.

ON UNKNOWN LEARNING
(De Ignota Litteratura)

by

JOHN WENCK

ON UNKNOWN LEARNING
(*De Ignota Litteratura*)[1]

19   To the venerable and devout man, Lord John of Gelnhausen,[2] formerly abbot in Maulbronn, intercessor for one of his own.

Most lovable Father, I was recently presented with *Learned Ignorance*, which consists of three books (each incomplete in itself) and which is written in a sufficiently elegant style. It begins with the words "*Admirabitur, et recte, maximum tuum et iam probatissimum ingenium*" and ends "*Eo aeternaliter fruituri qui est in saecula benedictus. Amen.*" Having looked over [this work], I feel called upon to write *Unknown Learning*. Here—by means of [a view] opposed to the points which the aforementioned *Learned Ignorance* deals with (in my judgment, harmfully) in regard to God, the universe, and Jesus Christ— an entrance opens unto the powers of the Lord so that we may be mindful of His justice.[3] Those who lack the knowledge of this justice have disobediently established their own, as the apostle says in Romans 10.[4] The promise of eternal life will perhaps lighten the burden of this work which I have undertaken. [This promise] concerns the repayment of supererogation (Luke 10)[5] and was made by God to the clarifiers of truth—[made] in what is written in Ecclesiasticus 24: "Those who explain me shall have eternal life."[6]

From an innate desire for health the minds of my readers will be vigilant with regard even to this *Unknown Learning*. With spiritual weapons, however, I am going to rebut certain statements from *Learned Ignorance*—[rebut them] as being incompatible with our faith, offensive to devout minds, and vainly leading away from obedience to God. At the head of what must be said comes the [command] in Psalms 45 ("Be still and see that I am God")[7] as being the legitimate enlistment of all our mental activity. For if I behold the mind of the prophet: after the elimination of malevolent wars, which are repugnant to our God, and, moreover, after the weapons of treachery have been broken[8] and
20   knowledge is to be had of Christ, our peacemaker and defender, then comes the command "Be still and see that I am God." For He envisioned certain who were free to spend time in the Lord's vineyard and who are accused in Matthew 20: "Why do you stand here all day idle?"[9] Very many *see*—not unto salvation, the end of our faith, but with regard to curiosity and vanity. [We

read] about these [individuals] in Romans 1: "They became vain in their thoughts, and their foolish heart was darkened."[10] The Lord God desires to remove, exclude, and separate us from these. Turning our leisure and our sight back toward Himself, He commands us—in order that we may behold with quietude—to be still. [The point is] not (1) that [we be still] in the sense of remaining in a mere cognitive seeing, which puffs us up (from which cognitive seeing even the demons derive their name in Greek, for "demons" means "those who know"), but is rather (2) that by directing our unbusied sight unto that which is truly God, we may have satisfying rest from all our commotion. Therefore, having beautifully prescribed *being still*, He added expositively, "and see." And He attached, explanatorily, what is supposed to be seen: viz., "that I am God." Here "I" singularizes and openly excludes every creature from the Divine Nature—distinguishing God from every creature, since God is Creator, not creature. Therefore, the whole exercise of busying our mind with *Unknown Learning*—[an exercise] necessary with respect to the struggle of making an inroad against *Learned Ignorance*—is governed by this verse.

This man of learned ignorance glories, telling the Cardinal that at sea, on his return from Greece, and being guided by supernal light, he found what he formerly had striven after by way of various doctrinal paths. And further specifying that which he found, he says: . . . *in order that I might embrace—in learned ignorance and through a transcending of the incorruptible truths which are humanly*[11] *knowable—incomprehensible things incomprehensibly.*[12] He says that *thanks to Him who is Truth he has expounded this [learned ignorance] in three books*. Yet, that disciple whom Jesus loved exhorts us, in his first letter, chapter 4, not to believe every spirit but to test the spirits [in order to determine] whether they are from God. And he adds the reason why this is necessary: "because many false prophets have gone out into the world."[13] Of which prophets the apostle, in II Corinthians 11, says, speaking more specifically: "[they are] false apostles, deceitful workmen, who transform themselves into apostles of Christ."[14] Among whose number is, perhaps, this man of learned ignorance, who under the guise of religion cunningly deceives those not yet having trained senses. For the teachings of the Waldensians, Eckhartians, and Wycliffians have long shown from what spirit this learned ignorance proceeds.

In Mark 1 we are commanded by the Savior to believe the Gospel,[15] for it is the indissoluble word of God (John 10: "Scripture cannot be broken").[16] In Galatians 1 the apostle gives Scriptural teaching precedence over an angelic proclamation: "Although we or an angel from heaven preach to you anything other than what we have preached to you, let him be accursed."[17] Now, the Gospel says in I Corinthians 13 that we understand through a mirror [and] in a symbolism.[18] How, then, in this life would we incomprehensibly apprehend what is incomprehensible? For in this life—in which, according to Boethius,[19] "everything which is received is received in accordance with the mode of the receiver"—it is impossible for man to comprehend in any other way than comprehensibly and in terms of an image. For [as we learn] from *De Anima* 3 the image is to the intellect that which color is to sight.[20] Now, it is evident that without the objectively activating light of color, sight cannot see anything; therefore, neither does it happen that we understand without an image. Accordingly, Holy Scripture has taught us through symbolisms that which is divinely inspired and revealed—also [doing so] conformably to the usual manner of our natural conception.

But in order to escape all calling into question of his arguments, this author of *Learned Ignorance* resorts to the following strategem: viz., [he asserts] that in incomprehensibly embracing such deep and incomprehensible matters, *the whole effort of our human intelligence elevates itself unto that Simplicity where contradictories coincide.*[21] And he says that the conception of his first book labors with this [task]. He calls this Simplicity *God*—not understanding that which the verse stated: viz., "that I am God," with whom no created thing coincides and with whom nothing from the nature of anything is mingled. Now, if the aforesaid teacher of learned ignorance wants in this way to prevent all opposition, then there will be no contradiction there. And who will refute him, since in that case no inference could be established? For there would be no inconsistency between an antecedent and a consequent opposite to it. What, then, would become of the inferences of our Savior's prophets, evangelists, and apostles by which our faith is seen to be in no small measure confirmed against the infidels? Moreover, such teaching as this author's destroys the fundamental principle of all knowledge: viz., the principle that it is impossible both to be and not to be the same thing,[22] [as we read] in *Metaphysics* 4. But this man cares little for the sayings of Aristotle. For he says that he *always sets out from [one and] the same foundation* and that he *has elicited, beyond the usual approach of the philosophers, [teachings which will seem] unusual to many*. Wherefore, [allegedly], the Lord Jesus has been magnified in his understanding and affection through an increase of his faith.[23]

Now, he says that his own foundation is the following [principle]: viz., *that with regard to the most simple and most abstract understanding all things are one*;[24] wherefore, it is necessary that *there* all things lose all differentiation. I have collected into theses and corollaries, because of the better possibility of their being remembered, the points elicited by him on the basis of this foundation. I will deal with them in sequence in what follows; but beforehand I will explain why I attached the title *Unknown Learning* to this writing.

Now, if we attend to our natural manner of learning, I agree in the first place with [what] the aforesaid author of *Learned Ignorance* [stated], in his prefatory explanation, with regard to the sensible aspect of the desire for knowing—viz., in the following passage: *just as a preceding unpleasant sensation in the opening of the stomach stimulates the nature for being restored, so wonder stimulates the desire-for-knowing which is naturally bestowed upon all human beings.*[25] For thus it is written in *Metaphysics* 1: "All human beings by nature desire to know."[26] And again: "Because of their wondering the ancients began to philosophize."[27] And I agree again with the oft-mentioned author of *Learned Ignorance* on the following point: [viz.,] that with regard to such a natural inclination for knowing, it is necessary that we open up a mode of scientific inquiry, or investigation, in order that [this inclination] may be put to use (so that it not be in vain but may attain rest in that object which is desired by the propensity of its own nature).[28] This [mode] is the following: *All those who make an investigation judge the uncertain proportionally—i.e., by means of a comparison with (or a relation, or proportion, to)*[29] *what is taken to be* (praesuppositi sive propositi) *certain.* [30] For this is the function of logic, which, as a mode of knowing, is said in *Metaphysics* 2 to direct and teach the mind to come, by means of inference, from the known to attaining a knowledge of the unknown.[31] Hence, all rational inquiry is comparative (*comparativa seu collativa*) and uses the means of comparative relation. Thus, each thing to be sought, pursued, or investigated comes to be judged and known from a proportional, or a comparative, reduction of what is uncertain, unknown, or unapprehended (which is being inquired about) to something taken to be certain, known, manifest, and apprehended, so that it becomes known and is manifested.[32] Hence, the beginning (*inchoatio sive inceptio aut initium*) of a rational inference is from what is known; and the end and goal is the manifesting of what is unknown. Therefore, in the title of his book he includes each of the two bounds of the inquiry, or inference: viz., "*docta,*" i.e., "what is known," and "*ignorantia,*" i.e., "what is unknown." I have done a similar thing in my book's title, which is "*ignota,*" viz., the *terminus ad quem* of this same intellectual investigation, and "*litteratura,*" viz., its *terminus a quo*.

This title has not been newly devised by me. Rather, it was enunciated formerly by the divinely inspired holy prophets; for in Isaiah 29 [it is said that] "a sealed book will be given to one who does not know letters;"[33] and in Psalms 70 David states that he does "not know learning" but nevertheless "will enter into the powers of the Lord" and "will be mindful of God's justice alone."[34] For by the testimony of Isaiah this unknown learning—[an unknowing] which repels human teachings—causes wisdom to perish from the "wise" and will conceal understanding from the "prudent"[35] whose works are in the dark (Isaiah here beautifully said, "whose works are in the dark"[36]). For what is done badly in the arts is not the fault of the art, which is light and knows no defect; rather, it is the fault of the man who acts badly, whose conduct is not in light but in darkness.[37]

On Unknown Learning

From these initial observations, then, the aforementioned author of *Learned Ignorance* is sufficiently shown to have a zeal [*emulatio sive zelus*] for knowing; but [the discussion] which follows will show that [this zeal is] not according to knowledge.[38]

Indeed, he says that knowing is not-knowing,[39] although possession and privation are distinguished [by him]. In fact, in the *terminus ad quem*, in which there is rest, privation was banished; for the advent of privation was inconsistent with possession.

He says further: *Only in the most learned ignorance* (doctissima ignorantia) *do we see most simple Being itself, which is the Essence of all things.*[40] *Wherefore, on the basis of what has previously been established: acquired knowledge* (docta notitia) *includes comparative relation, and consequently [it includes] number and finitude. But these have no place in most simple Being itself—because, as infinite, it escapes and transcends all comparative relation.*[41] *For since most simple Being itself cannot be comparatively greater and lesser, it is beyond all that we can conceive.*[42] *And so, since a transference is made from what is finite to what is most infinite and most independent of all figure,*[43] *our ignorance will incomprehensibly teach [us]*[44] *about this thing. [For our ignorance] will leave behind sensible things,*[45] *which [this infinite thing] transcends, and will readily and incomprehensibly ascend unto the inapprehensible truth.*[46]

I answer him by reference to Wisdom 13: "By the greatness of the beauty of creation the Creator can be knowably seen."[47] Delighted with the beauty of creatures, David says in Psalms 91 that he sings "because You have given me, O Lord, a delight in Your work."[48] David does not here exclude or disdain [God's] work, or creation; and in the last Psalm he commands [us] to praise the Lord in His holy places.[49] So, then, the author of *Learned Ignorance*, entering into intense darkness and leaving behind all the beauty and comeliness of creatures, vanishes amid thoughts. Still being a pilgrim, and hence not being able to see God as He is, he does not at all glorify God. Rather, going about in his own darkness, he leaves behind and leaves aside the peak-of-divine-praise to which all psalmody is brought. Who among the faithful does not know that this is unbelieving and most impious? A meagerness of instruction in logic has led him to this error. In his own ignorance he thought that by way of logic he had received an adequate and precise comparative relation to God—[a relation which] would be a means for pursuing and knowing God.

I come now—through theses[50] and corollaries—more specially to his statements.

First thesis: *All things coincide with God.*[51] This is evident because He is the Absolute Maximum, which cannot be comparatively greater and lesser.[52]

Therefore, nothing is opposed to Him.[53] *Consequently, God—on account of an absence of division—is the totality of things, as Hermes Trismegistus says.*[54] Hence, too, no name can properly befit Him, because of the absence of a distinct bestowal; for the bestowal of a name is based upon the determinate quality of that upon which the name is bestowed.[55]

This thesis is alluded to by Meister Eckhart in the vernacular book which he wrote for the queen of Hungary, sister of the dukes of Austria—[a book] which begins: "*Benedictus Deus et pater Domini nostri Ihesu Christi.*"[56] [Here Eckhart] says: "A man ought to be very attentive to (1) despoiling and divesting himself of his own image and [of the image] of each creature, and to (2) knowing no father except God alone. [For] then there will be nothing which can sadden or disturb him—not God, not a creature, not any created thing or any uncreated thing. [For] his whole being, living, apprehending, knowing, and loving will be *from God, in God,* and *God.*"[57] And in his sermons he [says]: "In the soul there is a certain citadel which sometimes I have called the guardian of the soul, sometimes the spark [of the soul]. It is very simple—as God is one and simple. It is so simple and so beyond every measure that God cannot view [it] according to measure and personal properties. And if it were to behold God, then this would be evident: viz., that He [is beyond] all His divine names and personal properties, because He is without measure and property. Now, insofar as God is one and simple and without measure and property, insofar as He is neither Father nor Son nor Holy Spirit, He can enter into this one thing which I am calling the citadel."[58]

See what great evils swarm and abound in such very simple learned ignorance and such very abstract understanding. Wherefore, John, bishop of Strasburg, on the sabbath before the Feast of the Assumption of the Blessed Virgin Mary, in the year of our Lord 1317, conducted a trial against the Beghards and the sisters in his own city, who were claiming (1) that God is, formally, whatever is and (2) that they were God—not being distinct [from Him] in nature.

Moreover, there cannot be any proof of the adduced thesis. For proof of the thesis would completely abolish [the doctrine of] the Blessed Trinity, since according to this author of *Learned Ignorance* there is neither distinction nor opposition of relations in the Absolute Maximum, which is God. Thus, the persons would not differ in their divine properties; and, consequently, in this learned ignorance there would be not only a confusion of the divine persons but also an essential union of all things with God. This [consequence] is patently opposed not only to orthodox faith but also to the [author] himself, who later in his book tries to prove the Blessed Trinity by means of likenesses—which, however, his learned ignorance has separated [from God] and left behind. And if in this way there is a separation of all things from God—as he affirms in view of his most learned ignorance of the most simple Being [and] Essence of all things—how is it that in this first thesis he connects all things with God through coinciding?

26 The first corollary of this first thesis: *By means of*[59] *Absolute Maximality all things are that which they are, because Absolute Maximality is Absolute Being, in whose absence there cannot be anything.*[60]

Eckhart, in his work on Genesis and Exodus, alludes to this [point] in the following way: "Being is God. For if it were other than God: either God would not exist, or else if He did exist, He would exist from something other [than Himself]."[61] And he adds: "The Beginning wherein God created heaven and earth is the primary and simple *now* of eternity—i.e., altogether the same *now* wherein God dwells from eternity and in which there is, was, and eternally will be the emanation of His persons. Hence, when I was once asked why God did not create the world earlier, I replied: because He was unable to, since before there was a world, *earlier* neither could be nor was. How was He able to create earlier, since He created the world in the same immediate *now* in which He was dwelling?"[62]

Let those who err give heed to Wisdom 11: "You have ordered all things in measure and number and weight. For great power has always belonged to You alone; and who shall resist the strength of Your arm? For the whole world before You is as the least grain of the balance and as a drop of the morning dew . . . which falls upon the earth."[63] Therefore, this corollary would destroy the individual existence of things within their own genus. These things are sustained by the power of God (as the apostle says in Hebrews 1: "upholding all things by the word of His power"),[64] in order that they not pass away into nothing. Now, if they are sustained by God, then surely they are not God (i.e., not Absolute Maximality) but are something and not nothing and are distinct from God, their creator.

The second corollary of this first thesis of the same learned ignorance: *This Absolute Maximality contains all things in itself, and it is present in all things because it encompasses all things by its totality.*[65] *By comparison, nature, which is contracted, is the "unfolding"*[66] *(so to speak) of everything which occurs through motion.*

Those who universalize maintain—on account of the simplicity of the Universal Nature which they posit in reality—that in such a precise Abstraction [i.e., in Absolute Maximality] all things are essentially divine. But this [view] is inconsistent with the divine simplicity. And it introduces real composition into God from creatures—something which we should shudder to say, since the

27 eternal, infinite Perfection which God is does not have anything whereby it increases or decreases. For just as God does not decrease through an emanation, so He does not essentially superabound through a return, or reduction, of creatures to Himself.

John Wenck

The second thesis of the same doctrine of ignorance: *The precise truth is incomprehensible; for since it is infinite, it lacks comparative relation to what is presupposed as certain—[presupposed] in order to arrive at what is uncertain. Now, what is infinite is—insofar as it is infinite—unknown.*[67]

[This thesis is] especially surprising, since [the author] earlier[68] said that most simple Being itself, which is the Essence of all things, is seen in most learned ignorance—by which ignorance incomprehensible things are grasped incomprehensibly. Since the same most simple Being itself is seen to be precise Truth, how is it both incomprehensible and incomprehensibly graspable? Now, the basis for this thesis would abolish our knowledge of God. Therefore, let there be understood to be, in the sciences, the following double mode of determining: viz., (1) the mode of composition (i.e., descending from first things to last things by combining the second with the first, [the third with the second], and so forth), and (2) the mode of analysis (i.e., resolving what is caused into first causes, and resolving what is composite into what is simple). Now, the supreme and most simple Cause is God. Given that creatures are God's effect and that an effect bears the likeness of its cause, then, as is taught in Book One of the *Sentences*:[69] God is knowable in a vestige and in an image, becoming known by a mark of likeness of creatures [to Him]; for through Scripture God is described for us by the likenesses of creatures [to Him]—[described] as besuits our understanding, [described] in the way in which He can be understood on [this pilgrim's] pathway. Hence, the precise truth—by virtue of its being precise—bears a relation and a proportion to other, non-precise truths (just as Absolute Maximality does to those maximalities which are concrete in their relations). Nor is it necessary to have, in the case of a cognitive intermediary [i.e., of an image or a likeness], a precise comparative relation, because that would be an identity rather than a likeness.

The first corollary of this second thesis: *There cannot be found two or more things which are so similar and equal that they could not be progressively more similar ad infinitum.*[70] *This is obvious from the degrees of equality in terms of which one thing is more equal to a second thing than to a third, in accordance with generic, specific, spatial, causal, and temporal agreement and difference among similar things. [Consider] the example of an [inscribed] polygon in relation to an [inscribing] circle.*[71]

This corollary destroys the status of causes and the distinction of beings within their own genus. According to the *Categories*, equality is based on quantity, and similarity on quality.[72] Now there is seen to be both quantity of mass, or magnitude, and quantity of power; and powers are finite, according to Book One of *On the Heavens*.[73] Likewise, each of the categories [is limited] by its own respective most general bound and its own respective most specific bound (as Porphyry teaches).[74] Therefore, how can [the man of learned ignorance] affirm that one thing is, *ad infinitum*, [progressively] more similar or more equal [to another]? For even [degrees of similarity and equality] are distinguished in relation to a maximum and a minimum, according to Book One of the *Physics*.[75] Nevertheless, from a comparison of any given thing with any other thing, an important foundation is provided for representational [*intentionalis*] memory, about which there is discussion elsewhere.[76]

The second corollary of the same second thesis: *A finite intellect cannot by means of likenesses precisely attain the truth about things, because there always remains a difference between the measure and the measured—no matter how equal they are.*[77]

It is clear, for Aristotle, (1) that the things which we know are the smallest parts of the things which we do not know, and (2) that our intellect discerns by means of an image and a likeness, and (3) that the equality and the likeness cannot be made an identity, but (4) that, nevertheless, the difference which remains in the things which are compared with one another does not destroy knowledge.[78] This means that through a likeness the intellect cannot precisely and wholly attain to the truth. And what is it to say this, other than (1) to acknowledge that [the intellect] understands the truth mediately rather than immediately—[an admission] which is suitable to philosophy and theology—and (2) to acknowledge the weakness of our cognitive power?

The third thesis of [this] same doctrine of ignorance: *The quiddity of things, which is the truth of beings, is unattainable in its purity.*[79] For the understanding can always be purified and refined ad infinitum.[80] I have just finished saying[81] that our intellect conceives the truth of things by means of an image and a likeness (for the possible intellect, according to *De Anima* 3, is the place of intelligible species);[82] and earlier I stated, by means of what was then said, that to see a thing in its purity and as it is pertains not to this life but to the heavenly life.[83] But this man of learned ignorance aims to understand a thing in its purity—[to understand it] by way of this same learned ignorance and apart from all likeness.[84] Notwithstanding, the quiddity, or truth, of things is intelligible even now. For since that-which-a-thing-is is the object of the intellect (according to *De Anima* 3),[85] there is a natural movement of the intellect unto it. But if it were unattainable, then this intellectual movement would be without a *terminus ad quem*. Consequently, there would be no end of the motion; and hence the motion would be infinite and in vain. This would be to destroy the intellect's proper operation.

Moreover, the reason in support of the thesis cannot be accepted. For the understanding will not be able to be altogether separated from a component of the material determination of knowledge (according to Book One of *Posterior Analytics*)—viz., from the following determination: that there is a cause of the knowledge.[86]

John Wenck

The first corollary of this third thesis: *In the unqualifiedly Maximum not only does the Minimum coincide [with the Maximum] but also all contradictories whatsoever are harmoniously combined, connected, and united.*[87] *This point is obvious. [For] since [the Maximum] is all that which can be (i.e., is actually all possible things), it is, in complete actuality, whatever is; and in this [actualized Maximum] there are not degrees of comparatively greater or lesser, nor is there opposition.*[88]

O how far the poison of error and falsehood is here disseminated! For this corollary destroys all scientific procedure and all inference—destroying, as well, all opposition and the law of contradiction. Hence, [it destroys] Aristotle's entire doctrine; for the basis of every doctrine has been destroyed. ([I spoke] about this point above.)[89] Nor is what is taken as the reason in support of [the thesis] valid: viz., that God is whatever is. For if God were whatever is, then neither heaven nor earth nor the other creatures would by His creating have proceeded from nothing into existence; but in Genesis the Lawgiver Moses teaches a view opposite to this [inference].

The second corollary of the same third thesis: *It is not, as well as is, all that which is conceived to be.*[90] *This is evident since the Absolute Maximum is a given thing in such way that it is all things; and it is also no thing.*[91]

To be sure, this corollary destroys [the doctrine] that God exists. For since God is conceived, [it follows that] He is not, as well as is. Moreover, in the supporting reason he teaches that God is a creature. Accordingly, this teacher of learned ignorance fails to be still and (in accordance with the commandment of the previously cited verse) to see what God says: viz., "that I am God." On the contrary, he is more foolish than formerly were the Beghards of Strasburg, who were condemned by their bishop. They used to say (1) that they were God and were not distinct [from Him] in nature, (2) that all the divine perfections were in them, and (3) that they were eternal and [were dwelling] in eternity. They also used to affirm (4) that they had created all things, (5) that they were more than God, and (6) that they needed no one (neither God nor any deity), saying: "If you wish to worship God, worship me."

The fourth thesis of the same learned ignorance: *That spiritual matters (which are unattainable by us in themselves) can be investigated symbolically has the following basis: viz., that all things bear a certain comparative relation to one another ([a relation which is], nonetheless, hidden from us and incomprehensible to us), so that from out of all things there arises one universe, and in [this] one maximum all things are this one. For the likeness of the original is the same—in oneness of nature—as the original.*[92]

O how great a weakness of intellect it is to assert that all things are one and that all things are essentially divine, and not to be able to distinguish an image

On Unknown Learning

from the original of which it is the image! Indeed, since the image is an approximate likeness of the original and does not come close to being an identity: it is not the same—in oneness of nature—as the original. Thus, the Lollards of Strasburg, who were condemned, used to say that a man can be united to God in such way that his ability both to will and to do everything is the same as God's. Indeed, Eckhart says in his sermons: "The Father begets His Son in me"; and "I am there that same Son, not another Son."[93] All of these [teachings] are so to be abominated that a faithful intellect will shun dealing with them except for defending its professed faith.

First corollary of the fourth thesis: *When we set out to investigate the unqualifiedly Maximum symbolically, we must leap beyond simple likeness.*[94] *This is evident because the Maximum cannot be any of the things which we either know or conceive, for it is undifferentiated and precise.*[95]

This corollary aims to understand God without a likeness and nevertheless (according to the supporting reason) does not aim to understand God. But this involves a contradiction. Accordingly the face-to-face vision of God—which vision he seems to mean by "leaping beyond likeness"—is reserved for the future state, [as we learn from] I John 3: Then "we shall see Him as He is."[96]

The second corollary of the same fourth thesis: *Our ignorance will teach [us]*,[97] *incomprehensibly, how we are supposed to think more correctly and truly about the Most High as we grope by means of a symbolism.*[98] *This is evident from the fact that ignorance is altogether independent of all figure and likewise transcends the forms* (rationes) *of finite and relational things.*[99]

31 How, I ask, can ignorance teach, since teaching is a positive act of instruction? Nor is the supporting reason valid, since to be freed of all form (*forma*) does not befit ignorance, which never had a form from which to be freed. Therefore, this corollary destroys all knowledge by exalting our ignorance above all knowledge.[100] Moreover, not even the supporting reason which he offers in chapter two of Book One is valid: viz., that *not-knowing is knowing, since Socrates seemed to himself to know nothing except that he did not know and also since every inquiry utilizes, for a knowledge of what is unknown, a comparative relation to what is known.*[101] For even the Teacher of the Gentiles—who judged himself to know nothing among the Corinthians[102] except Jesus Christ and Him crucified—did not deny other knowledge, in which he abounded. Instead, he offered the Corinthians the unknown learning of the sealed book, which is Christ Jesus.[103] Indeed, Socrates, in stating that he knew that he knew nothing, affirmed that he had knowledge. He denied that he had complete knowledge (i.e., he admitted that he had partial knowledge)—thereby implying that he desired to know what he did not yet know but was still ignorant of. For "he who increases (*apponit*) knowledge also increases sorrow,"[104] Ecclesiastes 1. (Or as the common translation has it: "he who adds

31

John Wenck

(*addit*) knowledge also adds sorrow"). For knowledge, acquired, causes a desire for greater knowledge, according to the passage in Ecclesiasticus 24: "those who eat of me shall still hunger."[105] How, then, could knowledge, which expels ignorance, arise from ignorance? For a privation is productive of evil, according to *Physics* 1.[106] From these considerations it is clear how much poisoning of knowledge and of practices has been introduced by this very abstract understanding (called *learned ignorance* or, in the vernacular, *living in detachment*),[107] in which there is a fading away of the senses and in which the glorifying of God is neglected. [This is the glorification] by which God is exalted among the heathen and on earth, according to the verse taken [as our text]: "Be still and see that I am God."[108] And there follows: "I will be exalted among the heathen, and I will be exalted on earth."[109]

The fifth thesis of the same learned ignorance: *Whatever is possible, this the Maximum is actually and maximally. [I do] not [mean] that it is from what is possible but rather that it is [what-is-possible] maximally.*[110] *This [fact] is evident from a comparative relation: viz., that an infinite line, [though a triangle], is not a triangle as [a triangle] is educed from a finite [line]; rather, [the infinite line] is* actually *an infinite triangle, which is identical with the [infinite] line. Hence, [by comparison], absolute possibility is, in the Maximum, not other than actually the Maximum.*[111] He says, further, that *all humanly apprehensible theology is elicited from this very great principle.*[112]

This thesis subverts every mode of theologizing which has been handed down to us throughout the entire Bible. For it says that from this principle (viz., that the Maximum is actually and maximally whatever is possible—from which principle it follows that being is the Maximum) there is elicited all humanly apprehensible theology. To support this principle, he has made many false assumptions, because no line is infinite, no triangle is a line, and possibility is not actuality. Therefore, it is not surprising if he infers false [conclusions] from false [premises]—given that, according to Book One of the *Physics*,[113] when one unacceptable point is granted, many others follow. Hence, from such statements of his it would follow that not only creatures which exist but also creatures which are possible would be God—[a conclusion which is] contrary to the verse taken [as our text]: "Be still and see that I am God."[114]

What else does this author of learned ignorance do, then, except lead men away from worship of God and from sincere and fitting devotion by saying[115] that he has been called and has been inflamed, even in faith, through a greater burning. Wanting to present such an aforementioned mode of theologizing, he exceedingly alienates men from the true mode of theologizing. Now, if Holy Scripture's mode of theologizing—a mode handed down from God—were set aside, would not the testimony given by the Savior about Himself in John 5 be nullified?: "Search the Scriptures. In them you think you have eternal life; and they are what give testimony of me."[116] Are we not exhorted in 1 Peter 2 to desire the milk of Scripture for the increase of our salvation?[117] Indeed, to those begotten in Christ this milk is so essential for salvation that the neglect of it leads to faithlessness. As the Savior says in Matthew 22: "You err, not knowing either the Scriptures or the power of God."[118] For if Holy Scripture is disregarded and if the powerful weakness of Christ is not regarded, then with respect to evident matters a man busies himself with images in which there is error, [as we see from] Galatians 5, where the apostle mentions heresies (*sectae*)—which in Greek are called *haereses*—as being among the works of the flesh which are to be detested. [119] For through the opposite [activity]—i.e., by our attending to the reading of Holy Scripture—(1) there is begotten a wisdom which dispels foolish images from these [men], and (2) the whole church is strengthened by Christ's weakness, which is God's strength and is stronger than all men,[120] and (3) there arises a new life in Christ, of whom ([according to] John 1) Moses wrote in the law and the prophets.[121]

33 The first corollary of the same fifth thesis: *The Maximum is not this thing and is not any other thing; rather, it is all things and not any of all the things.*[122] *This is evident because the Maximum is the being of all things.*[123]

This corollary—viz., that the Absolute Maximum is all things and is not any of all the things—involves a contradiction. For any of all the things is something, since nothing neither composes nor constitutes a creature, which has been brought forth by means of creation, and since (according to John 1)[124] all things have been made by the Word, without which there is nothing.

The second corollary of the same [fifth thesis]: *In learned ignorance elegance of words is deemed folly, and wisdom is deemed ignorance*[125] *because these bear a connecting but limited comparative relation [to each other].*[126]

Behold a confused man, walking about in darkness, who by means of a perverse comparative relation by which he was supposed to ascend unto understanding walks the pathway to foolishness and to foolish ignorance!

The third corollary: *There is not found to be any other precise measure of every essence than the Essence of the unqualifiedly Maximum.*[127] *This is evident because all other [measures] can be more precise and more absolute.*[128]

See where his own abstract knowledge leads this author of learned ignorance! For if God (as he supposes the essence of the unqualifiedly Maximum to be) is the precise measure of every essence, then how will it be the case that He exceeds, incomparably, every essence? And how will the following [doctrine from] *Metaphysics* 10 remain standing?: "In each genus a first thing is the measure (*metrum et mensura*) of the subsequent things of that genus; hence, in each genus there is a proper and precise measure."[129]

John Wenck

The sixth thesis of the same learned ignorance: *In order that, in God, the trinity and the oneness may be more clearly conceived to be the same thing, or that the distinction [may be more clearly conceived to be] not other than the indistinction, the following is necessary: to embrace, in a simple concept, contradictories (as far as possible) and to precede them and [embrace them as] one in their own very simple Beginning, viz., the unqualifiedly Maximum.*[130] *This is evident because in this [Beginning] distinction and indistinction are not other [than each other], but indistinction is distinction, and plurality is oneness*[131]*—just as Parmenides said that God is He for whom to be anything which is is to be everything which is.*[132]

By this thesis the author shows clearly that he is a man of learned ignorance. For just as a feigned holiness is a double abomination (since it is the feigning of what does not exist), so this learned ignorance (which is a feigned existence of knowledge, i.e., is a nonexisting knowledge) has a false appearance of knowledge, and therewith a lack of knowledge.[133] And so, this learned ignorance of his will be a double ignorance, or twofold unknowing, which I shall thus attempt (as best I can) to hedge and surround with reasons to the contrary—lest (considering the verse in Ecclesiasticus 36: "Where there is no hedge, the possession will be despoiled")[134] in accordance with his inordinate desires for knowing he deceive the world. For if this thesis of his is not enclosed by sound doctrines, it will eliminate distinction in God and will abolish the trinity (which, anyhow, he tries to show to be identical to the oneness). For plurality arises from distinction; and all things are identical in God if no opposition of relation opposes [this identity].

His supporting reason for this thesis is especially lame: viz., that God is He for whom to be anything which is is to be everything which is. For according to the author [of the *Book*] *of Causes*,[135] the First Cause, too, is present in any given thing—in addition to the presence of what is mingled with this thing. Perhaps various undigested perusals of ancient books have deceived this learned-ignorant author.

The first corollary of the same sixth thesis: *In such an unqualifiedly maximum the angles or the triangles cannot be numbered through one, two, three.*[136] *For each angle or triangle is in each other angle or triangle (as the Son says, "I am in the Father and the Father in me"). And they all are one maximum—through which maximum we get beyond all opposition.*[137]

To one who knows philosophy, it is evident that when a triangle is said to be in a quadrangle, or the sensitive to be in the intellectual, the mode of being is other than when the Son is said to be in the Father. Therefore, take counsel of the apostle: "do not be led away by various and strange doctrines" (Hebrews 13).[138] And the reason is added: "For it is best to establish the heart with grace, lest it wander about in accordance with its adulterous lusts for diverse doctrines."

The second corollary of the same [sixth thesis]: *In the oneness of the Trinity the identity is so great that it precedes even all relative oppositions.*[139] *This is evident because in the Trinity* other *and* different *are not opposed to* identity. *For since the Maximum is of infinite oneness, all the things which befit it are it without difference and otherness.*[140] *Hence, it is not Father, not Son, and not Holy Spirit. For it is only infinity—not [an infinity] which begets or is begotten or proceeds.*[141]

He speaks expressly against the Athanasian Creed, in which the following is said: "In this Trinity there is nothing earlier or later." Moreover, he abolishes [the view that] the Trinity is essentially God *ab aeterno*.

The third corollary of the same [sixth thesis]: *Because God is the enfolding of all things, even of contradictories, then since nothing can escape His foresight, all things related to God's foresight are necessary.*[142] *This is evident because in God all things are God, who is Absolute Necessity. And so, it is necessary that God foresaw what He foresaw. For if unfolding is posited, enfolding is posited.*[143] *Now, in His simplicity God enfolds the totality of things. Hence, even the name "tetragrammaton" (i.e., from four letters, viz., Yod, Heh, Vav, and Heh—which name befits God according to His own essence) signifies [God] as One-and-all, or All-in-one.*[144] *By comparison, the now enfolds time; and time is an ordered [series of] now[s]. And rest is a oneness which enfolds motion; and motion is the unfolding of rest, or rest ordered serially.*[145] *Similarly, for the Father to beget the Son was [for Him] to create all things in the Word.*[146]

This corollary is pernicious, because it eliminates the contingency of future events—contrary to the Philosopher in *De Interpretation* 9.[147] Moreover, it deifies all things, annihilates all things, supposes that annihilation is deification, and maintains that to generate the Son and to create creatures are the same.

Seventh thesis: *The creation always existed, from the time it was able to exist; for the creation is God's being.*[148] *Who, indeed, can understand that God is the Form of being and nevertheless is not mingled with the creation*[149] *but is one enfolding of all things?*[150] *For God is the enfolding of all things in that all things are in Him; and He is the unfolding of all things in that He is in all things*[151]—*just as, by way of illustration, number is the unfolding of oneness, and just as a point is the perfection of magnitudes, identity the enfolding of difference, equality [the enfolding] of inequality, and simplicity [the enfolding] of divisions.*[152]

This thesis destroys [the status of] the creation; for a condition of the creation is that the creation has not always existed. Moreover, since God Himself always exists, how can the creation be God's being? For although the First Good is desired formally (*exemplariter*) in every good, nevertheless the First

36 Good is not augumented from creatures. As David says to the Lord: "You have no need of my goods."[153] For as "all the rivers flow into the sea, and, yet, the sea does not overflow" (Ecclesiastes 1),[154] so nothing from creatures adds to the divine perfection.

A corollary of the same [seventh] thesis: *The plurality of things arises from the fact that God is present in nothing.*[155] This is evident because take away God from the creation and nothing remains[156]—*just as when a single face [which appears] in different mirrors is removed, none of the images remain.*[157]

This corollary deprives God of His own being—since, in nothing, being is nothing.[158]

The second corollary: *The Absolute Quiddity of the sun is not other than the Absolute Quiddity of the moon.*[159] This is evident because it is God Himself who is the Absolute Being and Absolute Quiddity of all things.[160]

This corollary is most abominable because it both confounds the quiddities of things and declares that God is the Quiddity of all things.

The third corollary: *Although the universe is neither the sun nor the moon, nevertheless in the sun it is the sun and in the moon it is the moon.*[161] This is evident because "universe" bespeaks a oneness of many things; hence, in the many the universe is these many.[162]

This corollary is incompatible with every philosophy.

Eighth thesis: *In the universe each thing is the universe; nonetheless, the universe is in each thing in one way, and each thing is in the universe in another way.*[163] This is evident because in each thing the universe is that which this thing is contractedly.[164] For in each creature the universe is this creature, just as in Socrates humanity is Socrates.[165]

This thesis not only expressly contradicts the third corollary of thesis 7 but also implies a contradiction, since an integral part is not the whole. As for his example that the greatest contracted line is contractedly all figures: he does not know what he is talking about. For he is adducing the mathematical entities of his very abstract understanding—[mathematical entities] made concrete by means of images.

The first corollary of the same eighth thesis: *The world-soul is the unfolding of the Divine Mind.*[166] This is evident because all things—which in God are one Exemplar—are, in the world-soul, many distinct [exemplars].[167] Consequently, God is the center point, as it were, and the world-soul is the circle, so to speak.[168]

37 Notice that he introduces an essential complexity into the soul. But the philosophers are of quite differing opinions regarding the soul.

Second corollary: *Absolute Motion is rest and is God, because Absolute Motion enfolds all motions, which rest unfolds,*[169] *as a circle [unfolds] a center.*[170]

On Unknown Learning

This corollary does away with [the doctrine of] the First Mover—contrary to [the view of] the Philosopher in Book 8 of the *Physics*.[171]

Ninth thesis: *God is the center of the world, of the earth, of all spheres, and of all things in the world; likewise, He is also the infinite circumference [of all things]*.[172] *This is evident because God alone is Infinite Equality*.[173] [The author] adds that *the earth is a noble star greater than the moon*.[174]

This thesis contradicts our knowledge of the heavens. Nor has the added comment ever before been heard.

First corollary: *God is Absolute Brightness, in whose blazing splendor all existing things endeavor, as best they can, to participate. [This Brightness] is contracted materially in all stars and immaterially in the life of things which are alive with an intellective life*.[175] This is evident because "*God is light, in whom there is no darkness*."[176]

This corollary detracts from the divine majesty. And in the supporting reason we see clearly that the author of learned ignorance accepts a likeness for a reality.

Second corollary: *The absolutely Maximum is actually and absolutely all possible things, and for this reason it is absolutely and maximally infinite; similarly, the maximum which is contracted to a genus and a species is actually [all] possible perfection in accordance with the given contraction*.[177] *An example is of a maximum line, with which a point coincides*.[178] *And so, God is the contracted maximum as well as the Absolute Maximum; and He enfolds creatures of all perfections*.[179]

This corollary makes possibility and actuality identical—contrary to the Philosopher, in *Metaphysics* 9.[180]

Third corollary: *The contracted maximum, which enfolds in itself the entire perfection of that contraction's nature, adds nothing to Absolute Maximality*.[181] *This is evident because Absolute Maximality is not other or different, since it is all things*.[182]

This corollary makes the creature equal to the Creator.

Fourth corollary: *Jesus embraces all creatures*.[183] *This is evident because Jesus is the maximum human being—in whom, because He is God, all things exist. He enfolds the living as well as the dead, just as corporeal light is the basis* (hypostasis) *of all colors*.[184]

Here I could use [against] this author of learned ignorance the words of Blessed John in Revelation 3: "You are wretched and miserable and poor and blind and naked. I counsel you to buy gold, fire tried, in order that the shame of your nakedness may not appear. Anoint your eyes with eyesalve, in order that you may see."[185] For he lacks eyesalve, since he does not understand Christ's humanity, which is the salve of our eyes for seeing the glory of God—as states the Hammer of Heretics, Blessed Augustine, when he deals with the following verse in John 1: "The Word was made flesh, and we beheld His glory."[186] Thus, by its cunning craft this corollary exceedingly dishonors Jesus by universalizing Him.

Tenth thesis: *God—in equality of being all things and without any change in Himself—exists in oneness with the humanity of the maximum [man], Jesus.*[187] *This is evident for the following reason: since God is of supreme equality and simplicity, then qua present in all things, God is not in them according to degrees—as if communicating Himself by degrees and by parts. But since none of these things can exist without [its respective] difference of degree, all things are in God according to themselves with a [respective] difference of degree. Therefore, even the maximum human being, Jesus, can exist in God only maximally.*[188]

This abominable thesis asserts an equality-of-being between divinity and humanity. It also maintains that God is not simple but composite, because of the difference in degree of all the things which exist in Him distinctly and with some degree.

First corollary: *Since the humanity of Christ is maximum, it so encompasses the complete possibility of the species that it is equality-of-being for each man. [It is] such [equality-of-being] that it is most specially united to each man, and Christ Himself is this very man by means of a most perfect union—each's numerical distinctness being preserved.*[189] *This is evident for the following reason: the maximality of human nature causes those who are one with Jesus to have merited whatever He has merited by His suffering; and yet, the difference in degree of merit is preserved, in accordance with the different degree of each [man's] union with Christ through faith formed by love.*[190]

39 How great the poisonousness of this corollary! For it destroys [the doctrine of] the individuality of Christ's humanity—i.e., [it teaches] that Christ was not an individual man but was universal man. It calls His humanity God—not on the basis of the hypostatic union but on the basis of a very abstract understanding. And it assumes that the being of Christ is the being of each man. From the fact that the human species as a whole [is each man], it assumes that Christ too is each man; and thus each man would be Christ. And what is the most dangerous thing of all: it ascribes Christ's merit to the maximality of human nature (Christ Himself not freely justifying us, who are the enemy of grace).[191] And as much as it can it stifles the justice of Christ. It is not able to say with the prophet: "Because I do not know learning, I will enter into the powers of the Lord; I will be mindful of Your justice alone."[192] For it ascribes no merit to the justice-of-Christ, from whence comes our every merit. And, furthermore, it states that we have merited what Christ merited. And then it appends [the

On Unknown Learning

statement] about love, so that it adds to its iniquity by means of a certain apparent color of religious faith. For the following differ greatly from one another: (1) the specific union of human nature, (2) the hypostatic union of the human nature with the divine nature in Christ, and (3) the affectional (*affectualis sive caritativa*) union of the mind with God. About this latter union the apostle in I Corinthians 6 [says]: "He who is joined to the Lord is one spirit."[193] Being ignorant of this difference of unions, the author of learned ignorance does not prove anything. And thus he so impiously confuses the order not only of natural things but also of the things of grace. For he is ignorant of nature; and he turns from grace unto the counsel of the wicked.

Second corollary: *As united with the divinity, the humanity of Jesus is fully absolute.*[194] This is evident because in this regard [Jesus's humanity] was free from time and was beyond time and was incorruptible absolutely and was the temporally contracted truth of the body. [His humanity was] "a sign, an image, and a shadow," as it were, of the supratemporal truth of the body. When this humanity was removed through death, Jesus remained—in the resurrection—in a supratemporal body. And His humanity was inseparably rooted on high in the divine incorruptibility.[195]

This corollary is altogether noxious in itself because it destroys [the doctrine of] the true humanity of Christ. For if in accordance with His humanity the man Christ had a soul and human flesh (as the Athanasian Creed states), then how can the humanity of Christ be fully absolute? Nor does the supporting reason remain standing, because the humanity-of-Christ which was assumed by the Word was not free from time. For (by the testimony of the apostle) "when the fulness of time was come,"[196] Christ was sent. Therefore, His humanity was not free from time. Nor was it above time and incorruptible absolutely; for in that case Christ would not have been truly dead. Moreover, in such a supporting reason [this author] denies the truth of Christ's body[197] and denies the resurrection of His body—[denies them] by universalizing Christ's humanity. (This universalization was fallaciously suggested to him by his own abstract understanding.) In this way he deprives us of the freely given benefits of Christ which are most graciously exhibited to us in Christ's temporal humanity.

Third corollary: *Christ and all men have the same humanity, though the numerical distinctness of the individuals remains unconfused.*[198] This is evident because there is only one indivisible humanity, which is the specific essence of all human beings. Hence, the humanity of all the human beings who—whether temporally before or after Christ—either have existed or will exist has, in Christ, put on immortality, so that after their resurrection they also will be eternally incorruptible.[199]

A remarkable corollary! The first part of it identifies all men individually and implies a universal, real thing multiplied with identity. But this [doctrine] is erroneous because only to the Divine Nature is it befitting to be multiplied hypostatically, or personally, in identity of nature.[200] However, the second part of [this] same corollary contradicts the first; i.e., [the corollary teaches] that the humanity of Christ and of all human beings is the same and yet is numerically and unconfusedly distinct.

Fourth corollary: *Each of the blessed having the truth-of-his-own-being preserved, exists in Christ Jesus as Christ; and through Christ [each exists] in God as God.*[201] *This is evident because "church" bespeaks a oneness of many [members]—each of whom has his personal truth preserved without confusion of natures or of degrees.*[202] *Moreover, the ecclesiastical union coincides on high with the hypostatic union of the natures in Christ. Furthermore, this latter union coincides with the Absolute Union, which is God.*[203] *For Christ is faith and love.*[204] *In His faith all true faith is included, and in His love all true love is included—though distinctions of degree always remain.*[205]

This corollary assumes (1) that each blessed one is Christ and God and (2) that faith and love are Christ. Moreover, by distinguishing different things in terms of degree, it continually confuses them. Thus, by distinguishing, he confounds—as is typical of someone of learned ignorance. He shows that he does not know anything at all about the different unions of things. Moreover, he speaks most deviantly about the church; and he substantially transforms into the nature of Christ the virtues (in particular, faith and love), which are accidents of the first species of quality.

I do not know whether in my whole lifetime I have ever seen a writer as heinous as this one when it comes to the issue of the divinity and the trinity of the Persons, the issue of the universe of things, the issue of the incarnation of Christ, the issue of the theological virtues, and the issue of the church. Now, whoever says[206] that from this learned ignorance he himself is more intensely inflamed with desires is presumably speaking about the infernal inflammation of the indomitable, unbridled tongue and of vain religion—about which James 3 [speaks].[207] With all your might flee from him, venerable Father, lest your senses (being seduced by this pseudo-apostle and deceptive writer who transforms himself into an apostle of Christ—seduced as by the cunning Serpent) be corrupted and fall away from the purity and simplicity of faith which is in Christ Jesus our Lord.[208] To His honor and glory I decided thus to write this *Unknown Learning* for your Devout Religiosity. Together with God the Father and with the Holy Spirit He lives as eternally blessed. Amen.[209]

A DEFENSE OF LEARNED IGNORANCE
(*Apologia Doctae Ignorantiae*)

by

NICHOLAS OF CUSA

A DEFENSE OF *LEARNED IGNORANCE*
FROM ONE DISCIPLE TO ANOTHER

(Apologia Doctae Ignorantiae Discipuli ad Discipulum)

Our common teacher, master Nicholas of Cusa, now added to the College of Cardinals, once told me how well you understand the coincidences which he disclosed to us in the books of *Learned Ignorance* (presented to the Apostolic Legate)[1] and in many of his other works. [He spoke of] your ardent wish to gather together everything which here and there flows from him regarding these matters. [He also reported] that you do not allow any of the learned men to pass by you without talking with them about this approach. [And he mentioned] that you have induced many who had despised this study to break for a short while with their long-standing habit of laboring with the Aristotelian tradition and to give themselves over to *these* considerations, in the faith that something important lies hidden therein—[to give themselves] to the extent that with an inward relish they become more deeply attracted and come to realize that this approach differs from others as much as sight differs from hearing. You have influenced many of these detractors in such way that together with you they behold with the mind's eye all secrets—[behold them] in the manner in which [this seeing] is progressively granted to a man. Therefore, since you are so eminent: I, a fellow-disciple of the same man, thought it right that there be brought to your attention certain points capable of misleading those who are not fully instructed; and [I thought that] you would know how to oppose such scoffings the more easily.

Today there came into my hands a treatise by a certain man who is not only undiscerning but also extremely arrogant—a man by the name of John Wenck, who calls himself a teacher of theology. To this treatise he gave the title *Unknown Learning*. After I read in it the grave reproaches and wrongs against our teacher and his books of *Learned Ignorance*, I went to our teacher—my mind distressed with great displeasure. I stated the reason for my coming and described the content of the reproaches.

The Teacher smiled for a moment and then, looking at me with an eye of affection, said: "Do not be troubled, Friend, but thank the Creator, who gave you so much light that you excel this man in wisdom as Socrates excelled the intelligentsia of his day."

I asked in what respect Socrates had excelled the Athenians. He replied: "In that he knew that he was ignorant, whereas the others (who were boasting that they knew something important, though being ignorant of many things) did not know that they were ignorant. Accordingly, Socrates obtained from the Delphic Oracle the attestation of his wisdom."

And I: "Tell me, I ask, O Teacher, how did Socrates' knowledge compare with that of the others?"

And he: "It was as the knowledge of the sun's brightness on the part of one who sees is to the knowledge of the sun's brightness on the part of one who is blind. For a blind man may have heard many [reports] about the sun's brightness—even that its brightness is so intense that it cannot be comprehended. [And he may] believe that on the basis of what he has thus heard he knows something about the sun's brightness; however, he remains ignorant of this brightness. By contrast, if one who has sight is asked regarding the sun's brightness "How bright is it?" he answers that he does not know. Moreover, he knows that he does not know; for since light is perceived by sight only, he knows by experience that the sun's brightness excels [the power of his] sight."

In this way [the Teacher] likened unto blind men very many of those who boast that they have a knowledge of theology. "For almost all who give themselves to the study of theology spend time with certain positive traditions and their forms; and when they know how to speak as do the others whom they have set up as their instructors, they think that they are theologians. They do not know that they are ignorant of that 'inaccessible Light in whom there is no darkness.'[2] By contrast, those who by means of learned ignorance are brought from hearing to mental sight rejoice at having attained, by more certain experience, a knowledge of their ignorance."

3

He said that a similar thing is found in Philo (that very wise man, to whom some authorities ascribe the books of Wisdom) in Question 51 of *Questions on Genesis*, where Philo speaks of Isaac's well.[3] In the words of the Teacher: "Just as those who dig a well seek water, so too those who pursue learning seek a summit. But [this summit] cannot be revealed to men. Now, certain conceited and mendacious individuals are accustomed to allege that they are the greatest musicians, the greatest grammarians, that they have transcended the heights of philosophy, the wisdom of all learning, and the limitations of virtue. But a wise, humble, and modest man openly admits how far he is from the summit. And one who takes an oath manifests, through such a bond, his awareness that a man cannot know anything perfectly. Whoever supposes that he knows so much about so many points will make bizarre statements. For the summit of knowledge is reserved only for God, whom the soul calls as a witness to the fact that with a pure conscience it is confessing its ignorance. For by itself the soul knows that it knows nothing unfailingly." The Teacher [said] these things.

A Defense of Learned Ignorance

4   I liked this comparison of the Teacher's. But I remarked that, as a consequence, true theology cannot be committed to writing. He openly acknowledged that everything either written or heard is vastly inferior to true theology; however, he maintained that true theology is hidden in sacred Scripture. For theology deals with the Kingdom of God; and our teacher Christ, by [His example of] a hidden treasure, stated that this Kingdom is hidden.[4] Thus, since every inquiry aims at, and searching the Scriptures involves, finding that which, when found, is hidden and remains hidden and inaccessible: he said it to be sufficiently evident that this [finding of what remains hidden] is not other than learned ignorance. "Very many teachers of our day," he said, "who possess the field of the Scriptures (where they have heard that the treasure of the Kingdom of God is hidden), boast that therefore they are rich—as does that man who wrote *Unknown Learning*. But whoever has recognized that the treasure remains hidden from the eyes of all the wise glories in the knowledge that he is poor. And he sees that in knowing he is poor—something the others do not know [about themselves]—he is richer than they. Accordingly, because he knows of his poverty he humbles himself; but the other, because of his presumed riches, vaunts himself—even as this ignorant man, inflated with the vanity of verbal knowledge, does not hesitate in his exordium to promise to elucidate eternal wisdom."

Thereafter, I, who was in a hurry to nullify what was written in *Unknown Learning*, began to ask who this former Abbot of Maulbronn was, through whom *Learned Ignorance* had been delivered to our adversary.[5]

The Teacher replied that the Abbot was a man of keen intelligence and of holy conduct who cherished the books of *Learned Ignorance*—especially because the Apostolic Legate and very many other great men praised them for
5   containing something important. Indeed, the Abbot was bound to this Legate by most singular affection. [The Teacher] added his belief that the Abbot had not given these books to this man [Wenck] but to another religious, from whom they had then come to Wenck. He further stated that in the dispute between the Apostolic See and the Council of Basel—a dispute which was being carried on through [a series of] diets—the Abbot had urged as true the cause of the Apostolic See, to which cause Wenck was opposed. The Teacher showed me the Adversary's words at the end of his compilation, where he calls the Teacher a pseudo-apostle.[6] ([He showed me this] so that I would see that this man spoke from emotion. For you know, dearest Friend, that no one resisted the men of Basel with so much fervor as our teacher.) Thus, this Wenck, who deviated from all the teachers [*doctores*] of the University of Heidelberg and took up the condemned cause of the men of Basel (in which cause he presumably is tenaciously continuing), was not ashamed to call the Defender of the truth a

pseudo-apostle. For he was concerned to make him hateful, and of little moment, to the Abbot and all others. But the deceitfulness did not prevail, for the truth triumphed.

But having read aloud to the Teacher the charges made by the adversary of *Learned Ignorance*, I saw him groan momentarily. When I inquired more closely about his reason, he answered: "If anyone studies the more important sages of antiquity, he finds that they took great precautions that mystical [teachings] not come into the hands of the unlearned. We read that Hermes Trismegistus gave to Asclepius, and Dionysius the Areopagite to Timothy, such an admonition.[7] And we know that even our Christ taught this; for He forbade the casting of a pearl (which is a figure of the Kingdom of God) before swine, in whom there is no intellect.[8] Thus, Paul declared that the things which he saw when caught up from this world into the third, intelligible heaven were not lawful to be revealed.[9] In each case there is a sole reason for this [prohibition and admonition]. For, indeed, where [a doctrine] is not understood, it not only fails to bear vital fruit but is despised and brings on death. [These sages] especially admonished [us] to beware lest a mystery be communicated to minds bound by the authority which long-standing custom possesses. For so great is the strength of long-established observance that many people's lives are erased sooner than their customs, as we experience with regard to the persecution of the Jews, the Sarracens, and other obdurate heretics who assert as a law—which they prefer to their lives—an opinion which has become established by prolonged acceptance. But the Aristotelian sect now prevails. This sect regards as heresy [the method of] the coincidence of opposites. (Yet, the endorsement of this [method] is the beginning of the ascent unto mystical theology.) Hence, this method (*via*), which is completely tasteless to those nourished in this sect, is pushed far from them, as being contrary to their undertaking. Hence, it would be comparable to a miracle—just as it would be the transformation of the sect—for them to reject Aristotle and to leap higher."

The Teacher said these things; but I did not immediately grasp or record them all. However, I did immediately suggest that while I read aloud *Unknown Learning* he arouse his mind to refuting this work. But he seemed to me to be sluggish and slower than I wished. For it did not seem to him that that writing was of such significance that it was suitable either to be read or to be reproached. As an attestation that a serious man ought not to attend to the refutation of the ignorant, he adduced what the great Dionysius writes in chapter 11 of *The Divine Names*.[10] There Dionysius says the following: because Paul stated that God cannot be ignorant of Himself,[11] he was reproached by Elymas the magician on the grounds that he had denied that God is omnipotent. When Dionysius proposed to reproach Elymas, he, Dionysius, admitted to being greatly afraid that he would be ridiculed as being someone

A Defense of Learned Ignorance

mindless who endeavored to demolish the buildings of boys-at-play—buildings
7 which are fragile and are built upon the sand. Dionysius called [such a demolisher] an imitator of inexperienced wrestlers, who often persuade the weak to become their adversaries, who vigorously fight in mock battle against absent [opponents], and who constantly beat the air with useless blows. They suppose that they have conquered their adversaries; and they proclaim themselves victors even though they do not even test the strength of these others. The Teacher said that this was properly analogous to what was being proposed [by me]. But I added (and he did not object but even conceded) that Dionysius had refuted the evil inference of that magician.

Thus, I overcame his kindness. And so that we might at least get started, he permitted me to read aloud rapidly. I read the exordium—[reading] from the words of David: "Be still and see that I am God."[12] And I continued with this section—[reading] that *God wills to remove our leisure*[13] *and that He commands our sight to be redirected unto Himself. Not remaining in a mere cognitive seeing, which puffs us up (from which cognitive seeing, he says, demons derive their name in Greek), but instead by directing our unbusied sight unto that which is truly God, we may have satisfying rest from all our commotion. For He says "I am God." Here "I" singularizes and openly excludes every creature from the Divine Nature—distinguishing God from every creature, since God is Creator, not creature.*[14] Thereafter, [our adversary] concludes with these words: *The whole exercise of busying our mind with* Unknown Learning—[*an exercise*] *necessary with respect to the struggle of making an inroad against* Learned Ignorance—*is governed by this verse.*[15]

When [I had read all of these statements] the Teacher, having with his hand enjoined silence, said in a gentle voice: "He put forth these points as a shield, but without having sufficiently reflected upon them in advance. For to a sound intellect all of them are consistent with *Learned Ignorance*. This man seems to have read few things and not to have understood the things he did read. For mystical theology leads to a rest and a silence where a vision of the invisible
8 God is granted to us. But the knowledge which is exercised for disputing is knowledge which looks for a victory of words and which is puffed up. It is far removed from the knowledge which approaches God, who is our peace. Hence, since [our adversary] proposes to hold a dispute—[a dispute] arising out of his knowledge—he could not conceal what kind of knowledge this was. For that which puffs up and arouses to conflict manifests itself—[showing] that it is not (as is learned ignorance) knowledge which, by means of rest, tends toward mental seeing. Now, he thought that he had disclosed something new when, from out of his inflating knowledge, he states what is meant in Greek by "*daemones.*" But presumably he has not examined Plato or Apuleius (*On the God of Socrates*) or Philo (who said that Moses called *angels* those whom the

Greeks called *demons*, even though in Greek good demons and evil demons are distinguished).[16]

"But when he adds that by means of the pronoun 'I' the prophet singularized God and excluded and distinguished Him from every creature (in which regard, he says, his own undertaking is confirmed), he seems to establish his view quite naively. For no one was ever so foolish as to maintain that God, who forms all things, is anything other than that than which a greater cannot be conceived.[17] Accordingly, God is not this or that—not the sky or the earth. Rather, He is the Bestower of being upon all things—so that He is, properly speaking, the Form of every form. And any given form—since it is not God—is not, properly speaking, form; for it is formed by the uncontracted and absolute Form. Therefore, no being can be absent from the most absolute, most perfect, and most simple Form, since this Form bestows all being.[18] And since all being is
9 from this Form and cannot be outside it, all being is in this Form. However, in this Form all being can be nothing other than this Form. For this Form is the infinite, most simple, and most perfect Form of being. Clearly, then, God ought in no respect to be conceived to have being in the manner in which something singular—which is different and distinct—is conceived to be. Nor [ought He to be conceived to have being] in the manner in which a universal or a genus or a species is conceived to be. Rather, [He ought to be thought to exist], beyond the coincidence of the singular and the universal, as the most absolute Form of all things generic, specific, and singular, and of all forms which can be conceived and spoken of. For Ineffable Form, which surpasses every concept, is the Beginning, the Middle, and the End of all such things.

"For suppose someone sees—beyond all knowledge of mathematics (which posits limits and measures for things) and beyond all plurality and number and harmonious proportion—all things apart from measure, number, and weight. Then, assuredly, he sees all things in terms of a most simple oneness. And to see God in this manner is to see all things as God and God as all things. But through learned ignorance we know that God cannot in this manner be seen by us. Now, if anyone sees all things in terms of number, weight, and measure, he sees hereby that that [which he sees] cannot be without difference and agreement. But since there cannot be otherness with respect to the Kingdom of God, in which there is a simplicity and peace that transcends all the senses, there is not [in God] singularity in the sense in which our adversary conceives it. Rather, [there is singularity] in the sense in which Avicenna (in his *Metaphysics* [in the section] on confirming the prophet) speaks about the singularity of God.[19] Here he admonishes against speaking to the people about this singularity because it would lead them astray rather than instruct them. For singular-
10 ity—in the sense in which he enjoins that it be kept concealed—is Singularity of singularities. And thus God is called unsingularly Singular—just as [He is also

called] infinite End, limitless Limit, and indistinct Distinction. For whoever directs his mind's eye toward the Absolute Singularity of all singulars sees clearly enough that Absolute Universality coincides with Absolute Singularity—just as the Absolute Maximum coincides with the Absolute Minimum, in which [Maximum-Minimum] all things are one. Hence, when by means of negative theology Avicenna attempts to ascend unto the singularity of God,[20] he frees God from everything singular and universal. But prior to Avicenna the divine Plato, in the *Parmenides*, more keenly made such an attempt to open a way to God. The divine Dionysius imitated Plato to such an extent that he is quite frequently found to have cited Plato's words in series. Nevertheless, together with Avicenna I concede that these [points] are not acceptable to an adversary who is from the common people and who distorts the loftiest prophetic visions into commonplace conceptions which are not representative of God. [In so doing, he proceeds] counter to the teaching of all the wise, including the great Dionysius, who in chapter 10 of *The Divine Names* (in Ambrose the Camadolesian's very recent translation, which we received from our most holy lord, Pope Nicholas) speaks as follows: 'Therefore, we must understand divine things not in a human manner but by going wholly outside ourselves and crossing over straightway unto God.'[21] There [he says] many things regarding this [point].

11   "Now you see, my friend, with how naive and weak a prop *Unknown Learning* is supported."

After our teacher, with regard to what had been read aloud, had thus given these replies point by point, I continued with the reading. From the subsequent passage[22] [I read about] our teacher's glorying over his having found, by the gift of God, that he was incomprehensibly led to incomprehensible matters by means of transcending things which are corruptible[23] and humanly knowable. After many abusive remarks (which did not disturb the Teacher), [our adversary] says that the gospel of I Corinthians 13, where he [viz., Paul] maintains that comprehension depends upon a mirror and a symbolism, contradicts this "finding."[24]

The Teacher enjoined me to stop for a moment and said: "See how a difference of sense arises when the respect is different. This man discerned, with respect to the mirror and the symbolism, that God—as He is [in Himself]—is incomprehensible. For in an image the truth cannot at all be seen as it is [in itself]. For every image, in that it is an image, falls short of the truth of its exemplar. Hence, it seemed to our critic that what is incomprehensible is not grasped incomprehensibly by means of any transcending. But if anyone realizes that an image is an image of the exemplar, then leaping beyond the image he turns himself incomprehensibly to the incomprehensible truth. For he who

Nicholas of Cusa

conceives of each creature as an image of the one Creator sees hereby that just as the being of an image does not at all have any perfection from itself, so its every perfection is from that of which it is an image; for the exemplar is the measure and the form (*ratio*) of the image. Now, God shines forth in creatures as the truth shines forth in an image. Therefore, if anyone sees that the very great variety of things is an image of the one God, then when he leaves behind all the variety of all the images, he proceeds incomprehensibly to the Incomprehensible. For he is led into an ecstasy when he gazes in wonderment at this infinite Being which in all comprehensible things is present as in a mirror and in a symbolism. He sees clearly that this Form, of which every creature is an

12 image, is not comprehensible on the basis of any created thing. (For no image can be an adequate measure of the truth, because in that it is an image it falls short.) Therefore, the absolute truth is not comprehensible.

"If, then, we are somehow to approach the absolute truth, we must do this by means of some incomprehensible glimpsing—as in the manner of a momentary rapture—just as with the bodily eye we momentarily but incomprehensibly glimpse the brightness of the sun. [The point is] *not* that the sun is not maximally visible when sunlight by its own strength forces itself upon our eyes; rather, [the point is that the sun], because of its most excellent visibility, is invisible to our grasp. In a similar manner God, who is Truth, which is the object of the intellect, is maximally intelligible; yet, because of His superexcellent intelligibility He is unintelligible. Hence, only learned ignorance, or comprehensible incomprehensibility, remains the truer way for transcending unto Him."

And I: "Dearest Teacher, although the consideration which you disclosed in *Learned Ignorance* did not come to you by means of study but rather by the gift of God, you no doubt have consulted many of the ancient sages in order to see whether the same point shines forth in them all. Hence, I ask that if any of the things which you have read come now to mind, you state [them]."

And he: "I confess, O Friend, that at the time I received [this] thought from on high I had not examined Dionysius or any of the true theologians. But with eager steps I betook myself to the writings of the teachers, though I found only a revelation expressed in various symbols. For example, Dionysius says to Gaius that most perfect ignorance is knowledge;[25] and he speaks in many places about one's knowledge of his ignorance. And Augustine says that God is attained by

13 ignorance rather than by knowledge.[26] For ignorance removes, but understanding conjoins. But learned ignorance unites all the ways by which we can approach the truth. In his *Metaphysics* Algazel said elegantly, in regard to God: 'If anyone knows demonstratively the necessary impossibility of his apprehending Him, then he is a knower and an apprehender; for he comes to know that God cannot be grasped by anyone. But if anyone cannot apprehend,

and does not know (on the basis of the aforementioned demonstration) that it is necessarily impossible to apprehend God, then he does not know God. And all men are thus ignorant, except for the worthy, the wise, and the prophets—all of whom have profound wisdom.'[27] Algazel [said] these things.

"But Aurelius Augustine—expounding the word of Paul in Romans 8 ('We do not know what to ask for')—declared, after other things, how it is that we have learned ignorance: 'We know that what we seek exists; but we do not know what kind of thing it is. We have this "learned ignorance," so to speak, through the Spirit, who helps our infirmity.'[28] And after a few [other statements]: 'Since Paul says that the Spirit implores with unutterable groanings, he indicates that the unknown thing is both unknown and not altogether unknown. For if it were altogether unknown, it would not be sought with groaning.'[29] Augustine [said] these things.

"Therefore, we possess learned ignorance, without which God would not be sought. Previously, I wrote a treatise *On Seeking God* (*De Quaerendo Deum*). Read it; for you will there discover that although [God] is everywhere and is not removed from us (as Paul said to the Athenians when he converted Dionysius),[30] nevertheless we approach more closely to Him when we find that He has moved farther away.[31] For the better we grasp the Inaccessible's greater distance from us, the closer we come to [this] Inaccessibility."

14   Although after the Teacher had said these things in this way I did not yet have my fill of hearing such points, nevertheless when I considered that much still needed to be said, I did not allow him to cite the common teachers. For I stated that the illustrious [teachers already mentioned], together with those cited in *Learned Ignorance*, were sufficient for our purposes. He assented; and I hastened on. I read about our adversary's claiming that the Teacher had used a strategem (in order to escape all attack) when he indicated his intent to turn, in elevation of mind, unto that Simplicity, where there is coincidence of contradictories.[32] When [I had read this] the Teacher laughed and said:

"When he claims that there was added a strategem which precludes all attack on my writing, he shows that he is moved by an envy against my person. But when he alleges that both the fundamental principle-of-knowledge (which is enfolded in the principle 'every thing either is or is not') and all inference are destroyed,[33] he is misconceiving. For he fails to notice that learned ignorance is concerned with the mind's eye and with apprehension-by-the-intellect [*intellectibilitas*]—so that whoever is led to the point of *seeing* ceases from all discursive reasoning, and his evidence comes from sight. 'He bears witness to what he has seen'—as John the Baptist says of Christ and as Paul says of his own rapture.[34] However, whoever pursues truth on the basis of evidence from hearing—even as we are quite commonly led by faith, which comes as a result of hearing[35]—has need of inference. Hence, if someone were to make the following statement, he would not at all be speaking accurately: 'Since you say that the evidence from seeing is more certain because it proves apart from any rational consideration and any inference, then you are denying that the evidence from hearing and that all discursive reasoning are of any importance.'[36]

"So logic and any philosophical investigation do not attain unto seeing. Now, a hunting-dog makes use of the [capability of] inference with which he is endowed—makes use of it in regard to footprints and in relation to sensible experience—in order by this means to attain, at length, what is sought; similarly, each animal in its own way [makes use of the capability of infer-
15 ence]. (Accordingly, the most wise Philo said that reason is present in all animals, as Blessed Jerome relates [of him] in *De Illustribus Viris*).[37] By comparison, man [makes use of] logic. For, as Algazel states, 'we are naturally endowed with logic; for logic is the power of reasoning.'[38] Now, rational animals reason discursively. Discursive reasoning investigates and makes inferences. Inference is, necessarily, bounded by a *terminus a quo* and a *terminus ad quem*. And things which are opposed to each other we call contradictories. Hence, opposing and separate boundaries belong to inferential reasoning. Therefore, in the domain of reason [*ratio*] the extremes are separate; for example, with regard to a circle's definition [*ratio*] (viz., that the lines from the center to the circumference be equal): the center [of a circle] cannot coincide with the circumference. But in the domain of the intellect [*intellectus*]—which has seen that number is enfolded in oneness, that a line is enfolded in a point, that a circle is enfolded in a center—the coincidence of oneness and plurality, of point and line, of center and circle is attained by mental sight apart from inference (as you were able to read about in the books *De Coniecturis*,[39] where I also asserted that God is beyond the coincidence of contradictories,[40] since He is the Opposition of opposites, according to Dionysius).[41]

"Henry of Mechlin was once brought (as he tells us in *Speculum Divinorum*)[42] to seeing, in the case of intellectual things, the coincidence of oneness and plurality—a coincidence at which he very greatly marveled. But, as you have often heard, if someone realizes that understanding is, in equal measure, both a motion and a rest of the intellect (as, in the *Confessions*, Augustine says of God [that He is both motion and rest]),[43] then he frees himself more easily from other contradictories."

16   Having said these things, the Teacher then suggested that I consider the fact that learned ignorance elevates someone, in the way that a high tower does, so that he may see. "For being situated up there, he sees that which is being sought (through various inferences and in the manner of a tracker) by one who is wandering about on the plain. And he sees to what extent the seeker comes toward and recedes from what is sought. Now, learned ignorance, which

A Defense of Learned Ignorance

pertains to the high region of intellect, makes judgments in a similar way about rational inference."

After the Teacher had in this way made these statements, whose substance I believe you have heard from him at different times, I said: "Our opponent does not seem to have understood what you meant by 'coincidence of contradictories.' For, as you heard,[44] he ascribes to you (howbeit, falsely) the statement that the creature coincides with the Creator; and he attacks this claim."

To these [words] the Teacher [replied]: "I said that 'the sensual man does not discern the things which are of the Kingdom of God.'[45] And if emotion had not overpowered our adversary, he would not have falsified my writings. But, so it seems, he was set in his desire roundly to attack these writings. And because of this desire he is found to be a falsifier—both in regard to meaning and in regard to words. ('It is the custom of the most obstinate heretics to truncate the Scriptures,' maintain the Fathers of the Sixth Synod.)[46] For a lover of truth denies that any such doctrine comes from the books of *Learned Ignorance;* and any of the things which [our adversary] infers, the lover of truth would not accept in the manner in which [our adversary] infers them. Indeed, to say that an image coincides with its exemplar, and that what is caused [coincides] with its cause, is characteristic of a man who is unintelligent rather than of a man who is mistaken. For from the fact that all things are in God as things caused are in their cause, it does not follow that the caused *is* the cause—although *in the cause* they are only the cause, just as you have often heard regarding oneness and number. For number is not oneness, although every number is enfolded in oneness, even as the caused [is enfolded] in the cause. But that which we understand as number is the unfolding of the power of oneness. Thus, in oneness number is only oneness.

"However, I think that you have adequately discerned—from what you have eagerly read in the book *De Dato Lumine*—what I believe about this matter.[47] For whoever examines the mind of someone writing on some point ought to read carefully all his writings and ought to resolve [his statements on this point] into one consistent meaning. For from truncated writings it is easy to find something which by itself seems inconsistent but which when compared with the whole corpus is [seen to be] consistent. By way of an analogy: When a poisonous animal is viewed not as a whole but in terms of its separate parts, it seems to possess no beauty or goodness. But when the parts are related to the whole of which they are members, they are found to have their beauty and their goodness. For the whole, which is wholly beautiful, is composed of a beautiful harmony of the parts. In like manner, St. Thomas, in the *Contra Gentiles*, says that certain men—on the basis of the words of the great Dionysius—were led to say that God is all things.[48] [They were led to say this] because in *The Celestial Hierarchy* Dionysius maintains that God is the Being of all things.[49] But if they

had read all the works of the Areopagite, then they would surely have discovered in *The Divine Names* that God is the Being of all things in such way that He is not any of these things, since what is caused can never be raised unto equality with its cause.[50] I do not believe that this [fact about God] can be discerned otherwise than by means of learned ignorance. For example, God is present everywhere in such way that He is present nowhere (for he is not absent from any place who is not present at any place); thus, God is present at every place nonspatially, just as He is great without quantity. Similarly, He *is* every place nonspatially, every time nontemporally, and every existent nonexistently. But He is not on this account any existent thing, even as He is not any place or any time. And yet, He is all in all, even as the one is all things in all numbers.
18 For were the one removed, number could not continue to be;[51] for number can exist only through the one. And because the one is every number, (not numerically but by way of enfolding), it is not any number. For example, it is neither the number two nor the number three."

    Hereto I appended [the following request]: that leaving aside the superfluous matters the Teacher, rather, dispel the Adversary's delusions—something which, I added, could easily be done since, in the manner mentioned, they are founded upon a false assumption.[52] Whereupon, the Teacher enjoined me to dispel, at any rate, the more obvious delusions and to permit him to deal, insofar as possible, with the unobvious ones.

    Then, having the Adversary's text at hand, I read from the place where he declares it wrong (since possession and privation are not identical) to say that knowing is not-knowing.[53]

    Immediately interrupting the reading, the Teacher said: "I am amazed at why [this] man, who regards himself as of considerable importance, maintains that the foregoing point is stated in the foregoing way in the books of *Learned Ignorance*. For although the title of chapter 1 is heuristically stated as "How it is that knowing is not-knowing," it does not thereby assert that knowing is not-knowing—except in the manner in which [the matter] is there explained: viz., that [someone] knows that he does not know. In this chapter a very clear exposition is made regarding the knowledge of one's ignorance, just as we have also sufficiently discussed this topic above. At the beginning of the book *The Divine Names* the great Dionysius says that this knowledge is supreme and divine.[54] And he adds that this knowledge—in terms of which there is ignorance[55] of the Supersubstantial—surpasses every word and all meaning and must be attributed to [the gift of] God."[56]

    Hereafter I read how it is that he reproaches that part in which we are enjoined to leave behind sensible things through learned ignorance in order that we may come to the Incomprehensible.[57] [He bases his reproach] on the belief that this [injunction] runs counter to what is read in Wisdom, chapter 13: viz., that the Creator can be knowably seen from the greatness of the beauty of creation.[58] I stated that this was not at all injurious to the undertaking. For since there is no comparative relation of the creature to the Creator, no created thing possesses a beauty through which the Creator can be attained. But from the greatness of the beauty and adornment of created things we are elevated unto what is infinitely and incomprehensibly beautiful—just as from a work of craft [we are referred] to the craftsman, although the work of craft bears no comparative relation to the craftsman. I said, in addition, that our adversary ought rightfully to have been filled with shame when he added that the Teacher of learned ignorance had scorned creatures as not conducing to our knowledge of God.[59] For in the last chapter of Book One of *Learned Ignorance* [our adversary] finds it to be most sufficiently stated that all worship of God is necessarily founded on affirmative statements, although learned ignorance reserves for itself the judgment about what is true. Wherefore, I concluded that everyone easily discerns the perverse mind and the crudity of understanding of that man, when he says:[60] *So, then, the author of* Learned Ignorance, *entering into intense darkness and leaving behind all the beauty and comeliness of creatures, vanishes amid thoughts. Still being a pilgrim, and hence not being able to see God as He is, he does not at all glorify God. Rather, going about in his own darkness, he leaves behind the peak-of-divine-praise to which all psalmody is brought. Who among the faithful does not know that this is unbelieving and most impious?* And [our adversary] adds that *a meagerness of instruction in logic has led him [i.e., the Teacher] to this error. In his own ignorance he thought that by way of logic he had found*[61] *an adequate and precise comparative relation to God—[a relation which] would be a means for pursuing and knowing God.*

To these [charges] I [replied]: "These are the words of a lying and conceited man who knows no theology."

Having praised my statements, the Teacher added that with someone who is mad we ought to deal sparingly rather than heaping insults upon him. "For that with which [our adversary] finds fault is sought in learned ignorance—as in *The Mystical Theology* our Dionysius (whose feast we are celebrating today)[62] instructs us thus to ascend into darkness with Moses.[63] For God is found when all things are left behind; and this darkness is light in the Lord. And in that very learned ignorance we approach nearer to God, as all the sages both before and after Dionysius have attempted [to do]. Hence, the first Greek commentator on Dionysius said: 'Whoever desires to attain unto God seems to ascend unto nothing rather than unto something; for God is not found except by one who leaves behind all things.'[64] Such an individual is regarded by our adversary as vanishing when he leaves behind all things; but according to the first theologians, this individual can only *then* be carried away with Moses to the place where the invisible God has been dwelling.[65] Now, Dionysius calls [this] darkness a divine ray.[66] And he states that those (of whose number is our adversary) who are fastened to visible things and think that there is not anything existing supersubstantially above the objects available to the eyes and senses believe they can attain, by means of their own knowledge, unto Him who has made [this] darkness His hideaway.[67] Moreover, he counsels Timothy to beware lest any such ignorant men should hear these mysteries."[68]

And then because of his kindness our teacher enjoined me that I should, if possible, lovingly give [the following] counsel to our adversary since he is incapable of [grasping] these high intellectual matters: viz., (1) to impose silence upon his own mouth, (2) to esteem that which he cannot grasp (rather than to reproach it), and (3) not to believe that someone to whom God has not granted it can, by [making] an effort, ascend unto these mysteries. "But if he hopes to obtain grace in order to be brought from blindness to light, then let him read with discernment the previously mentioned *Mystical Theology*, Maximus the Monk, Hugh of St. Victor, Robert of Lincoln,[69] John the Scot, the Abbot of Vercelli,[70] and other more modern commentators on that book. Doubtlessly, he will realize that he has hitherto been blind."

Admiring the longsuffering of the Teacher, I added: "I cannot bear [our adversary's] comparing you to one who is ignorant of logic, as Averroes [compared] Avicenna."

Whereto the Teacher [responded]: "Do not let this annoy you. For even if I were the most ignorant of all men, I would at least be satisfied that I knew of my ignorance—whereas my adversary does not have this knowledge [of his ignorance], although he is without understanding. We find it written that Blessed Ambrose added to his prayers [the request]: 'Deliver us, O Lord, from the dialecticians.'[71] For a superabundance of logic is injurious, rather than beneficial, to very sacred theology."

And I: "Since you, O Teacher, tried to show that God cannot be known as He is (herein is the root of learned ignorance), why does our adversary foist upon you an untruth regarding exact precision?"[72]

Whereto the Teacher [replied]: "He speaks now in this way, now in that way. For he has read the books of *Learned Ignorance* only in order to confound (if possible) what is correctly expressed [in them]. Hence, he has understood nothing of what he has read. Thus, it happened that in reproaching what was not written as if it had been written, he confounded himself rather than doing injury to learned, sacred ignorance, which cannot be spurned by anyone who has apprehended it. For in all my works nothing is more clearly found than the contrary of that upon which he fastens. For had he wanted to, he could everywhere have ascertained that I believe only this: viz., that precision—as it

A Defense of Learned Ignorance

is—remains inaccessible to all. Nevertheless, I affirm that learned ignorance alone excels incomparably every mode of contemplating God, even as all the saints also teach."

I continued with the reading—[reading aloud the passage] where our adversary says:[73] *I come now—through theses and corollaries—more specially to his statements. First thesis: All things coincide with God. This is evident because He is the Absolute Maximum, which cannot be comparatively greater and lesser. Therefore, nothing is opposed to Him. Consequently, God—on account of an absence of division—is the totality of things. And no name can properly befit Him, because the bestowal of a name is based upon the determinate quality of that upon which the name is bestowed. Meister Eckhart alludes*[74] *to this [thesis].*

[Our adversary] adds that the bishop of Strasburg condemned those who were asserting (1) that God is, formally, all things and (2) that they were God—not being distinct [from Him] in nature.[75] Then, attacking the supporting reason, he says: if there were neither distinction nor opposition of relations in God, what would follow would be altogether absurd; for in that case the [doctrine of] the Trinity would be abolished, etc.[76]

Whereto the Teacher [responded]: "Should not this falsifier be ridiculed rather than refuted? Why does he not state the place where this thesis is found in the books of *Learned Ignorance*?"

And I: "He was unable to state [the place] because [this thesis] is nowhere found [there]. For I have read very carefully and do not recall ever having found [the statement] that all things coincide with God. (In the second [book] of *Learned Ignorance* I did indeed find [the statement] that the creation is neither God nor nothing.)[77] I do not understand what our adversary means; and perhaps he does not understand his own [meaning]. For I have found it to be necessary (and this is what I did [there] read) that all the divine attributes coincide in God and that all of theology is arranged in a circle, so that in God justice is goodness, and conversely, (and similarly for the other attributes).[78] All the saints who have considered the infinite simplicity of God agree about this point."

[And the Teacher]: "Nevertheless, [the doctrine of] the Superblessed Trinity is compatible with this [doctrine of the divine simplicity]. For the infinite simplicity allows that God is one in such way that He is three, and is three in such way that He is one—even as this [point] is explained more clearly in the books of *Learned Ignorance*.[79] (In like manner, we read that Pope Celestine, in professing his faith, spoke as follows: 'We confess our belief that the indivisible holy Trinity—Father, Son, and Holy Spirit—is one in such way that it is three, and is three in such way that it is one.')[80]

"See how it is that he who does not pay attention to the coincidence of unity

and trinity has no understanding at all regarding theological matters. Nor does it follow from this [doctrine of coincidence] that the Father is the Son or the Holy Spirit. To [this] stiff-necked man the following cannot occur: viz., that in the coincidence of supreme simplicity and indivisibility, of oneness and trinity, the person of the Father, the person of the Son, and the person of the Holy Spirit are distinct. Words whose significations are not compatible with theology hinder
24 him. For example, when we say that the Father is one person, the Son another person, and the Holy Spirit a third person, 'otherness' cannot retain its [ordinary] signification. For this word is under assignment to signify an otherness which is separate and distinct from oneness; and so, there is no otherness unless there is number. However, such otherness cannot at all befit the indivisible Trinity. Hence, a commentator on Boethius's *De Trinitate* ([a commentator who is] easily the most intelligent man of all those whom I have read) says: 'From the fact that there is no number in God, in whom trinity is oneness (in whom, as Augustine says, if you begin to number, you begin to err),[81] it follows that in God there is no *difference* in the proper sense of the word.'[82] ('In the proper sense of the word' means 'in accordance with the word's assignment.') Now, this [point about God] is better understood than it can be expressed, although it is never so perfectly understood that it cannot be more perfectly understood. Whoever desires to ascend unto the divine mode must rise above all imaginable and intelligible modes. For the divine mode, which is the Mode of every mode, is attained only above every mode. For nothing similar to it can occur to our mind—as Paul said most elegantly in Acts 17. For who can conceive of a mode which is indistinctly distinct?—as Athanasius says, 'neither confounding the persons nor dividing the substance.'[83] For all the [symbolic] likenesses proposed by the saints (including the most divine Dionysius) are altogether disproportional [to God]; and to all who do not have learned ignorance (i.e., a knowledge of the fact that [the likenesses] are altogether disproportional), [the likenesses] are useless rather than useful. However, in Book One of *Learned Ignorance* enough (though disproportionally less than could be said) is found stated about these matters—[stated] in the manner in which God has granted it."[84]

I, not permitting to remain undiscussed that which our adversary alleged about Meister Eckhart, asked whether the Teacher had learned anything from Eckhart.

25 The Teacher said that here and there in [various] libraries he had seen (1) Eckhart's many expository works on very many books of the Bible, (2) many sermons, and (3) many disputations. Furthermore, he had read many articles extracted from Eckhart's writings on John—[articles which were] criticized and rejected by others. And he had seen at Mainz, at the home of the teacher John Guldenschaf,[85] the short writing of Eckhart's in which he replies to those

A Defense of Learned Ignorance

who had attempted to reproach him, and in which he sets forth his own views and shows that the critics have not understood him.[86] The Teacher said, however, that he had never read that Eckhart thought the creation to be the Creator; and he praised Eckhart's genius and ardor. Yet, he wished that his books would be removed from public places; for the people are not suited for [the statements] which Eckhart often intersperses, contrary to the custom of the other teachers; nevertheless, intelligent men find in them many subtle and useful [points].

Thereupon I read the corollary which our adversary sets forth: viz., that *in*[87] *Absolute Maximality all things are that which they are, because [Absolute Maximality] is Absolute Being, in whose absence there is nothing.*[88] He adds that Eckhart too maintains that being is God;[89] and he infers therefrom that the individual existence of things within their own genus is destroyed.[90]

Whereupon the Teacher said: "We might reply to our adversary what Augustine, in the *Confessions*, replied when he praised God as the source of all being, adding: 'What is it to me if you do not understand?'[91] For since we name God *Creator* and say that He exists: elevating ourselves unto coincidence, we say that God coincides with being. Moses names Him *Former*: 'Therefore, God formed man,' etc.[92] Therefore, if God is the Form of forms, He gives being—even though the form of earth gives being to earth, and the form of fire [gives being] to fire. Yet, the Form which gives being is God, who forms every form. Hence, just as (1) an image has a form which gives to it that being through which it is an image, and (2) the form of the image is a formed form, and (3) whatever truth [the image] has, it has it only from [that] form which is its truth and exemplar, so, in God, every creature is that which it is. For in God every creature—[each of] which is the image of God—is present in its Truth.[93] Nevertheless, the individual existence of things through their own forms is not thereby destroyed. If that man cared about the truth, he ought to have added—on the basis of what he could have found stated quite extensively, clearly, and distinctly in *Learned Ignorance*—the contrary corollary.

"The case is similar when [our adversary] mentions Meister Eckhart. For Eckhart, toward the beginning of [his commentary on] Genesis,[94] where he advances his views about being (after he has proved (1) that God is Being itself and is the one who grants being and (2) that particular forms are this or that being), adds that the individual existence of things through their own being is not therefore destroyed but instead is established. He proves this [point] by means of three illustrations: viz., matter, the parts of a whole, and the humanity of Christ. For matter is not destroyed and altogether reduced to nothing by virtue of the fact that the entire being of the whole comes from the form. Nor is the part [reduced to nothing] by virtue of the fact that the being of the part is completely from the being of the whole. And by virtue of our saying that in Christ there is only the personal, hypostatic being of the Word, we are not denying that Christ was a real man along with other men. ([Eckhart] there adds the reasons for this [thus illustrated point])."

Next, I read the other corollary: that *Absolute Maximality contains all things in itself and is present in all things.*[95] I added the adversary's statement: viz., that *those who universalize maintain that in such a precise Abstraction [i.e., in Absolute Maximality] all things are essentially divine.*[96]

27 Whereto the Teacher [replied]: "I do not know what he means by 'those who universalize.' We know from the Apostle Paul and from all the wise that God is in all things and that all things are in Him.[97] However, no one [who holds this position] thereby affirms that there is composition in God; for in God all things are God. For example, in God the earth is not the earth but is God—and similarly regarding each other thing. Hence, when that man infers that this [doctrine] is inconsistent with the [doctrine of] divine simplicity, he understands nothing at all. For just as it is not inconsistent with the simplicity of oneness that every number is enfolded in oneness, so [it is not inconsistent] with the simplicity of the Cause that everything caused [is enfolded in the Cause].

"And when he proclaims that infinite perfection cannot be made more perfect,[98] I admit it," said the Teacher. "Accordingly, all the perfection of all perfect things is, in God, God. He is the Absolute Perfection of all things, and He enfolds all the perfections of all things. For if there were positable a perfection which is not enfolded in Divine Perfection, Divine Perfection could be greater and would not be infinite."

See, dearest Friend and Fellow-disciple, how our teacher draws from the Adversary's reasoning an inference which opposes the Adversary.

Hereafter, I read aloud to the Teacher the second thesis which the Adversary extracted: viz., that precision cannot be comprehended;[99] and [I read about] his wonderment at how precision can be seen in learned ignorance if it cannot be comprehended.[100]

Then the Teacher added: "It is not strange that he might wonder; for nothing is more wondrous to a man than is learned ignorance, i.e., the seeing that precision cannot be seen—as, above, I sufficiently discussed this [point]. When he says that this foundation destroys the knowledge of God, he speaks the truth. For someone's belief that he knows some thing which cannot be known is not knowledge. With regard to such a thing, knowing is knowing that he cannot know.

28 "[Our adversary] stated a true corollary: viz., that all likeness is imperfect.[101] But when he wonders about how it is that (in the case of things which have limits to their magnitude) if a similarity is posited, then a greater similarity can always be posited *ad infinitum*:[102] let him consider the dividing of a finite line. For in this case we do not come to an indivisible point, even

though we seem to approach it through [dividing] the parts of parts.

"The other corollary is likewise true: viz., that truth is not attained by means of likenesses."[103]

Subsequently, I read the third thesis, which [our adversary] claims to have taken from *Learned Ignorance*: viz., that quiddity is unattainable.[104]

The Teacher said: "Although [quiddity *is*] intelligible, as he proposes (even as God is supremely intelligible and the sun supremely visible), nevertheless it is never actually understood. Nor from the coincidence of opposites in the Maximum does there follow—as our opponent infers—this *poison of error and falsehood*: viz., the destruction of the fundamental principle of the sciences, i.e., of the first principle.[105] For that principle is first with respect to discursive reasoning but not at all with respect to intuitive understanding—as I said earlier[106] about this [matter].

"Nor is it true, if God is everything which is, that He did not therefore create all things from nothing. For since God alone is the enfolding of all the being of every existent: in creating, He unfolded heaven and earth. Or better, since God is, by way of enfolding and in an intellectually divine manner, all things: He is the Unfolder of all things, the Creator of all things, the Maker of all things—and whatever [else] can be said concerning this [point]. This is the way the great Dionysius argues.[107]

"And if there were Beghards who made such statements as our adversary alleges (viz., that, in nature, they were God),[108] then they were rightfully condemned—just as Almericus too was condemned by Innocent III at a general council (about which [you may read] in the chapter *"Damnamus de Summa Trinitate"*). Almericus did not rightly understand that God is all things by way of enfolding; some of his errors are cited by John Andrea in *Novella*.[109] Men of little understanding chance to fall into error when they search out higher [truths] without learned ignorance. They are blinded by an infinity of supremely intelligible light in their mind's eye. And having no knowledge of their blindness, they believe that they see; and as if they were seeing, they become rigid in their assertions—just as the Jews, who do not have the Spirit, are by the letter led unto death.[110] Moreover, there are some men who—when they find in other men views to which they are unaccustomed (and especially when they find that these others believe themselves to be learned just in case they recognize themselves to be unknowing)—think that these others, who have sight and are wise, are really ignorant and erring. Hence, all the saints rightly admonish that intellectual light be withdrawn from those with weak mental eyes. Holy Dionysius's books, Marius Victorinus's *Ad Candidum Arrianum*, Theodorus's *Clavis Physicae*, John Scotus Erigena's *Periphyseos*, David of Dinant's books, Brother John of Mossbach's commentaries on the propositions of Proclus, and other such books are not at all to be shown to those [with such eyes]."

I subsequently read, in turn, the fourth thesis. The Teacher heard that in this thesis the Adversary claims [that the following view] comes from *Learned Ignorance*: viz., that there is a single nature for the image and the exemplar.[111]

Whereupon the Teacher cried out: "Far be it! Far be it! This is the detestable outrage of a shameless falsifier!" And seizing a copy of *Learned Ignorance*, he read from Book One, chapter eleven:

> The fact that spiritual matters (which are unattainable by us in themselves) are investigated *symbolically* has its basis in what was said earlier. For all things have a certain comparative relation to one another ([a relation which is], nonetheless, hidden from us and incomprehensible to us), so that from out of all things there arises one universe and in [this] one maximum all things are this maximum.[112] And although every image seems to be like its exemplar, nevertheless except for the Maximal Image (which is, in oneness of nature, the very thing which its Exemplar is) no image is so similar or equal to its exemplar that it cannot be infinitely more similar and equal. (These [doctrines] have already been made known from the preceding [remarks].

These [words are found] in that passage.

31 "Notice," said the Teacher, "that that falsifier alleges to be affirmed of every diminished image that which according to Paul is stated exclusively of the only begotten Son, who is the Image which is consubstantial with the Father."[113]

Whereto I, very greatly aroused, added: "Let this mendacious truncator of books go away now and hide himself. For he who offends against the light—something which I consider to be the sin against the Holy Spirit—is not worthy of the light."

After I had quickly read aloud the subsequent [points], the Teacher showed me how the Adversary used falsity and truncation and mendacity and perverse interpretation in regard to them all. And of the place where [the Adversary] tries to say about Socrates some things which he knows nothing of,[114] the Teacher remarked: "Let him look at Plato's book *De Apologia Socratis*, where Socrates pleads his own cause at the trial, and he will discover his own fantasies, which are devoid of all truth."

And I: "Concerning [this] grey-haired man of advanced age who regards himself as one of the intelligentsia: how astounding that he writes such puerile foolishness!—especially when he construes learned ignorance as a life of detachment."[115]

I asked whether something was to be said against the charge which the Adversary makes, in the fifth thesis, against the view that the Maximum is

A Defense of Learned Ignorance

actually every possible thing.[116] Whereupon [the Teacher] said that it is vain to contend with one who lacks understanding. "For since God is purest, infinite Actuality, He is absolutely everything which is at all possible; and in this coincidence is hidden all apprehensible theology. The Adversary does not understand what theology is or what he is attacking or what he is saying. For example, because it is stated in *Learned Ignorance* that 'God is not this thing and is not any other thing, but is all things and is not any of all things[117] (which are the words of Holy Dionysius),'[118] he says that the [expression] 'is all things and is not any of all things' is self-contradictory;[119] and he does not understand that in the mode of enfolding [God] is all things but that in the mode of unfolding He is not any of these things. And since [our adversary] does not have any understanding, he laughs when he reads very weighty words. He does not know that they are [the words] of the saints and that the one who explicated learned ignorance adduced them in order (in accordance with the instruction of Holy Dionysius) not to pass beyond the bounds of the saints.

"The same holds true for those things which are stated about measure in the third corollary of the fifth thesis and in the [immediately] subsequent [comments]. For he cannot grasp that the infinite is the most adequate measure of finite things—even though the finite is altogether disproportional to the infinite. Nor can he grasp the example about the infinite line. He charges this example with falsity.[120] But [he does so] in vain, because the impossibility of there actually being an infinite line is shown in many ways in *Learned Ignorance*;[121] however, by the positing of an infinite line the intellect is helped to make headway toward the unqualifiedly Infinite, which is Absolute Necessity of being."

[The Teacher] added that Augustine had attained, as follows, unto [the view] that God is measure: "God is in all things, but not through parts; rather, He is as a whole in all things—whether these things be great or small. Therefore, since He is equally in all things, He is the most equal Measure of every measure."[122] Hereby, however, Augustine does not deny the unendedness of that magnitude which is Absolute Magnitude.

"But when in the sixth thesis [the Adversary] attacks Parmenides, he is endeavoring to attack not only *him* but all the learned and holy theologians whom he does not at all understand. ([I spoke] above about this [point].)[123] And in his own way he afterwards states, most falsely, that the following [view] comes from *Learned Ignorance*: 'Because all the things which befit God are God, He is neither Father nor Son . . . etc.'[124] It is right to hold that in accordance with the consideration of infinity God is neither Father nor Son. For the consideration of God according to infinity occurs by way of negation; and so, in that case, all things are denied [of God]—even as Holy Dionysius, too, says this very thing in these very words at the end of *The Mystical Theology*.[125]

"When [the Adversary] attacks [divine] foresight,[126] he shows that he is totally ignorant. For that point (although it is very clearly made) is not understandable by such a perceptually oriented investigator as our adversary shows himself to be."

Because in the remaining theses [this] falsifier proceeds by at times adding what he did not find and at times affirming what was not affirmed, the Teacher, having become weary, wanted to turn toward more useful pursuits. Thus, I was constrained to pass more quickly over the Adversary's invective. But after I had rapidly read from *Unknown Learning* the theses which [the Adversary] says he excerpted from *Learned Ignorance*, the Teacher picked up a copy of *Learned Ignorance* and read the second and the third chapters of Book Two. And he showed clearly that the seventh thesis, together with its corollaries, was excerpted perversely. For in those chapters nothing is expressly dealt with other than [the view] that the being of creation derives from Absolute Being in a manner which can neither be expressed nor understood; there is no other assertion, although different modes of discourse are touched upon.

But [regarding] the place where the Adversary attacks [the view] that God is the Absolute Quiddity of all things,[127] the Teacher said: "That man understands nothing at all. For God is the Quiddity of all quiddities and is the Absolute Quiddity of all things—even as He is the Absolute Being of beings and the Absolute Life of living things. (The church expresses this in prayer: 'God, Life of living things,' . . . and so on.) To say this is not to confound or to destroy the quiddities of things but to establish them, as wise men recognize."

The Teacher did not care to comment on the other theses; and he scorned the ignorance of the Adversary. Nevertheless, I asked him to comment on the fact that the Adversary, with sheer impudence and in an abusive way, disdains him as being wretched, impoverished, blind, and empty of understanding.[128]

34 Whereto the Teacher [responded]: "I openly acknowledge all that he says about the blindness of the intellect." But [the Teacher] asserted that he excelled the Adversary in that he knew he was blind.

And [of the passage] where [the Adversary] charges that Jesus is dishonored,[129] the Teacher said: "The intent of *Learned Ignorance* is not that Jesus be dishonored but that He be magnified in our understanding and affection." But the Adversary, he showed, speaks as would someone who said [the following]: "If anyone were elevated to become a supremely majestic person—so that he were King of kings and Lord of lords (as Christ is elevated)—he would *thereby* be dishonored." Now, no one doubts that this statement is characteristic of a mad man.

Therefore, after the Adversary's writings had been compared with the text of

A Defense of Learned Ignorance

Learned Ignorance, and after it had been shown that the Opponent falsely elicited the asserted theses and either understood nothing of all [these matters] or, at least, chose to understand nothing of them (interpreting all of them perversely), the Teacher said: "What was written in *Learned Ignorance* about Jesus was written in accordance with Holy Scripture and in a manner which befits the goal that Christ increase in us. For in its own way *Learned Ignorance* endeavors to lead us to those [teachings] about Christ which were left to us by John the Evangelist, Paul the Apostle, Hierotheus, Dionysius, Pope Leo, Ambrose in his letters to Herennius, Fulgentius, and the other loftiest holy intellects. Nevertheless, *Learned Ignorance* falls short, as do all those intellects which have ever undertaken to describe that mystery."

35   Having turned toward me with a loving countenance, [the Teacher] said: "Friend, you know perfectly well that those who through the loftiness of faith pass beyond sensible things and are joined to Christ and to truth are held in contempt by the ignorant men of this world. For, as the great Dionysius testifies in chapter 10 of *The Divine Names*, 'he who is joined to the truth knows how he is well off, even if most [people] reproach him as having become mindless and beside himself.'[130] And [Dionysius says] that through their deaths the principal leaders have declared of the truth that it alone is the one and simple divine notion."[131]

Hence, with very great affection of heart [the Teacher] admonished me not to grow lukewarm in my fervent study [but to continue] until the point where I would be elevated unto simplicity of understanding, in order that I would better know the unknowable God (who through knowledge and ignorance is known in and from all things, as Dionysius attests in the same chapter)[132] and Blessed Jesus (who alone is the highest of all things, the perfection of all things, and the fulness of all things). And [he admonished] that through this studying I apply, to the degree granted, my mind's every effort to seeing that I am never worthy to understand anything. And he promised that if I in any way at all tasted the divine sweetness of so great a mystery of ineffable grace, then none of the sophists could ever confuse me.

"For by our every movement we seek only peace; and the Peace which surpasses all the senses is our peace (viz., the Life of our life); living from and in this Peace we are tranquil with inexpressible delight. Accordingly, everyone who apprehends [this Peace] will say with Paul: Who shall separate me from this true Life?[133] Not death—because as dying I live.[134] Therefore, nothing will separate you at [that] time when the most frightful of all frightful things will not frighten you. You will laugh at all the blind when they promise to show you Him whom they do not see; and you will cling to the embraces of Him whom your soul will love with all its might. To whom be glory forever."

36   This, O most lovable Fellow-disciple, is what I have remembered [as coming] from the Teacher's heart in defense of *Learned Ignorance*. Although many things have slipped from my memory, I transmit these things to you for reading and, where it seems to you needful, for communicating. [I transmit them] so that in your fervor there may grow that admirable seed by which we are elevated for seeing divine matters (just as I have long since heard that throughout Italy great fruit will be forthcoming from that seed which was received in studious intellects because of your solicitous cultivation). For this speculation will surely conquer all the modes of reasoning of all the philosophers, although it is difficult to leave behind things to which we are accustomed. Do not hesitate to let me continually share in whatever progress you make. For by this [means] alone—as by a certain divine nourishment—I am joyously restored. Here below, I continually aspire (through learned ignorance and according as God deems fit to grant) unto the fruition of that life which I now thus behold from afar and which I daily strive to approach closer to. May God, who is so greatly desired and who is eternally blessed, grant that we, being freed from the present condition, may by divine gift obtain this [fruition].

ABBREVIATIONS

PRAENOTANDA

CROSS REFERENCES

NOTES

ABBREVIATIONS

Ap.	Apologia Doctae Ignorantiae
DI	De Docta Ignorantia
DP	De Possest (text edited by J. Hopkins in PNC)
IL	De Ignota Litteratura
MFCG	Mitteilungen und Forschungsbeiträge der Cusanus-Gesellschaft (ed. Rudolf Haubst)
NA	De Li Non Aliud (text edited by J. Hopkins in his Nicholas of Cusa on God as Not-other: A Translation and an Appraisal of De Li Non Aliud. Minneapolis: Banning Press, 3rd ed. 1987)
NC	Nicolò da Cusa. Florence: Sansoni, 1962. (Pubblicazioni della Facoltà di Magisterio dell'Università di Padova)
NK	Nikolaus von Kues. Einführung in sein philosophisches Denken. Ed. Klaus Jacobi. Munich: K. Alber, 1979
PL	Patrologia Latina, ed. J.-P. Migne
PNC	J. Hopkins. A Concise Introduction to the Philosophy of Nicholas of Cusa. Minneapolis: Banning Press, 3rd ed. 1986
SHAW	Sitzungsberichte der Heidelberger Akademie der Wissenschaften. Philosophisch-historische Klasse. Heidelberg: C. Winter
M	Codex Latinus 190, Mainz, Stadtbibliothek
T	Codex Latinus 228/1467, Trier, Stadtbibliothek
v	E. Vansteenberghe, ed. Le "De Ignota Litteratura" de Jean Wenck de Herrenberg contre Nicolas de Cuse [Vol. 8, Heft 6 (1910) of Beiträge zur Geschichte der Philosophie des Mittelalters]. Münster: Aschendorff, 1912

Abbreviations in the Latin notes:

add.	addit; addunt
cf.	confer
coni.	conicit
corr.	corrigit; corrigunt
del.	delet; delent
in marg.	in margine
lin.	linea; lineam
om.	omittit; omittunt

PRAENOTANDA

1. The English translation of *IL* was made from the new edition of the Latin text, appended to the present volume. The translation of *Ap.* was made from *Nicolai de Cusa Opera Omnia*, Vol. II, edited by Raymond Klibansky (Leipzig: Felix Meiner Verlag, 1932). A number of references in the notes have also been adapted from this volume.
2. All references to Nicholas's works are to the Latin texts—specifically to the following texts in the following editions:
   A. Heidelberg Academy Edition: *De Coniecturis, De Deo Abscondito, De Quaerendo Deum, De Filiatione Dei, De Dato Patris Luminum, Apologia Doctae Ignorantiae, Idiota* (1983 edition) *de Sapientia, de Mente, de Staticis Experimentis, De Pace Fidei, De Venatione Sapientiae*.
   B. Heidelberg Academy Editions as found in the Latin-German edition of Felix Meiner Verlag's Philosophische Bibliothek: *De Docta Ignorantia, De Beryllo*.
   C. Banning Press Editions: *De Visione Dei, De Possest, De Li Non Aliud*.
   D. Strasburg Edition as reprinted by W. de Gruyter: all remaining Cusanus works, unless specified explicitly as Paris Edition.
   For some treatises the reference indicates book and chapter; for others, margin number and line; for still others, page and line. Readers should have no difficulty determining which is which when they consult the particular Latin text. For example, "*DI* II, 6 (125:19–20)" indicates *De Docta Ignorantia*, Book II, chap. 6, margin number 125, lines 19 and 20.
3. The margin numbers appearing in the translation of *Ap.* correspond to the page numbers in Vol. II of the *Opera Omnia*. And the margin numbers in the translation of *IL* correspond to the margin numbers in the new edition of the Latin text; they also correspond to the page numbers in the earlier edition published by E. Vansteenberghe. Insofar as possible the line lengths have also been made to correspond, so that all references to page and line of Vansteenberghe's edition can be treated as references to section and line of the new edition.
4. References to Aristotle's works include, in parentheses, the standard Bekker numbers as indicated in the Loeb Library editions of the Greek texts. However, since the Loeb Library volumes have more lines per Bekker page than do the Bekker texts themselves, an improvisation was necessary in citing. Accordingly, a reference such as "*De Anima* 2 (423^a23–24.2)" is meant to indicate not only lines 23 and 24 in the Loeb version but also the two lines following line 24 (both of which precede line 25 as marked in the Loeb margin).

Praenotanda

5. Any Latin words inserted into the English translations for purposes of clarification are placed in parentheses—except that nouns whose case has been changed to the nominative are bracketed.
6. References to the Psalms are to the Douay version (and, in parentheses, to the King James' version).
7. In the Latin text of *IL*, punctuation, capitalization, and spelling (except for proper names) are editorialized. In particular, the references to Scripture are editorialized.

CROSS REFERENCES

The following is a list of Wenck's references to *DI* and of Nicholas's references, in *Ap.*, to *IL*:

IL	refers to	DI
20:24–26		263:7–9
21:23–24		264:1–3
22:3–6		264:4–9
22:7–9		27:11–15
22:18–19		1:19–23
22:22–25		2:3–9
22:27–29		2:16–17
22:32–37		2:17–21
23:23		2:2
23:26–27		51:7–9
23:28–31		cf. 3:2–6
23:31–33		11:7–9
23:33–34		33:14–15
23:34–35		33:16
23:35–24:2		cf. 8:5–7
24:1		cf. 11:4–7
24:20		11:7–8; 12:12
24:21		5:8,11
24:22–25		cf. 75–76
26:1–3		6:1–2; 15:12–13; 15:17–18
26:27–28		6:6–8
26:28–30		153:1–4
27:4–7		2:16–17; 3:2–3; 9:2–3
27:20–21		cf. 30:4–7
27:29–31		9:14–15
27:31–28:2		9:10–13
28:2		10:9–13
28:13–15		10:1–2
28:15–16		9:16–17
28:26–27		10:18–19
28:28		10:6–8
29:9–11		12:18–25
29:12–14		11:13–15; 12:1–5

Cross References

IL	refers to	DI
29:24–25		12:7–8
29:25–26		12:10–11
30:3–9		30:7–17
30:21–23		33:6–7
30:23–25		33:4–6
30:31–33		33:16–18
30:34–35		33:14–15
31:7–8		4:3–4
31:8–9		2:16–18
31:29–31		42:8–10
31:31–34		42:11–14
32:1–2		43:6–7
33:1–3		43:13–16
33:3		51:7–8 (cf. 73:3)
33:9–10		44:7–8
33:15–16		46:10–12
33:17		46:12–13
33:22–24		47:12–14
33:25–30		57:11–20
33:30–31		57:16–17,21
33:32–33		71:1–3
34:18–20		58:3–4
34:20–21		58:4–5
34:21		58:6–8
34:22		43:3–4
34:30–31		63:10–11
34:32–34		63:11–14
34:34–35:2		87:7–11
35:6–8		67:6–9; 69:1–3
35:9–11		69:3–4,7,10–11
35:11–15		75:4–10
35:15–17		106:1–5
35:18		80:17–18
35:23		101:12–13
35:24		101:6–7
35:24–25		102:1–2
35:26		107:1
35:26–28		107:11–12
35:28–30		108:1–2; 107:6; 106:11–12
36:5–6		110:11–12

Cross References

IL	refers to	DI
36:6–7		110:12–13
36:7–8		cf. 111:15–22
36:11–12		115:5–6
36:12–13		115:6–7
36:16–17		115:13–14
36:17–18		115:16–17; 116:21
36:20–22		118:15–17
36:22–23		118:14–15
36:23–24		115:17–19
36:30–31		143:6–7
36:31–32		143:7–8
36:33–34		145:13–14
37:3–4		155:3–4; 106:2–3
37:4–5		145:14
37:8–10		157:23–26
37:10		157:22–23
37:11		166:1; 167:8–9
37:14–17		177:10–17
37:17–18		177:11
37:22–25		190:9–13
37:25–26		191:1–3
37:26–28		192:6–7; 191:13–14
37:31–33		191:8–11; 194:5–6
37:33–34		193:2–3
38:2		233:11–12
38:3–5		233:12–13,17–18
38:16–17		204:20–22
38:18–23		204:13–19,22–23
38:28–31		219:2–8
38:32–35		219:10–14
39:24–25		225:13–14
39:25–31		225:20–21; 226:2–4,8–13
40:11–12		227:15–16
40:13–17		227:12–13,17–22
40:25–27		260:12–14
40:27–28		261:1–3
40:29–31		262:4–7
40:31		257:9–10
40:31–33		254:20–22
41:11–12		264:7–9

Cross References

Ap.	*refers to*	**IL**
5:8		41:15
7:11		19:22–23
7:12–19		20:7–17
7:19–22		20:17–20
11:4–7		20:21–26
11:8–10		21:8–11
14:5–9		21:20–24
14:12–14		21:34–22:1
18:8–9		23:23–24
18:21–22		23:35–24:2
19:13–22		24:7–16
22:10–16		24:17–26
22:17–19		25:17–21
22:19–23:2		25:22–32
25:14–15		26:1–3
25:15–16		26:3–5
25:16–17		26:20–21
26:26–27		26:27–28
26:28–29		26:31–33
27:9		26:35–27:1
27:18		27:4–5
27:18–20		27:8–12
28:1		27:29–31
28:2–3		28:8–10
28:6–7		28:13–15
28:9–10		28:26–27
28:13–15		29:15–19
28:24–29:1		29:32–34
30:6		30:8–9. cf. 30:10–12
31:10		31:7–8,13–16
31:15		31:24
31:18		31:29–31. cf. 32:3–5
31:25–26		33:4–5
32:8–9		32:7–8
32:19		33:32–33
32:22–23		34:33–35:2
33:4		35:19–20
33:19–20		36:14–15
33:28–29		38:7–8
34:4		38:14

NOTES TO THE INTRODUCTION

1. *Ap.* 5:11-13. Wenck must have shown much courage in this regard.
2. The following list of Wenck's writings is taken from Klaus D. Kuhnekath, *Die Philosophie des Johannes Wenck von Herrenberg im Vergleich zu den Lehren des Nikolaus von Kues* (Cologne: University of Cologne Ph.D. dissertation, 1975), p. XV.
   Parva logicalia (presumably before 1426)
   De ymagine et similitudine contra eghardicos (1430)
   Principium zum 1. Sentenzenbuch (1431)
   Das Büchlein von der Seele (1436)
   Notes on Events at the Reichstag (1441)
   Epistola in causa schismatis (1441)
   Reply to John of Gelnhausen (1442)
   De ignota litteratura (1442-1443)
   Memoriale divinorum officiorum (1445)
   Paradigmata ingeniorum artis (no earlier than 1445)
   De facie scolae doctae ignorantiae (1449-1455)
   Commentary on *The Celestial Hierarchy* (1455)
   Sermo in die nativitatis Christi (1457)
   De consequentiis (no exact date possible)
   Commentary on Boethius's *De hebdomadibus*
   Commentary on Aristotle's *De anima* III
   Commentary on *Liber de causis*
3. G. Ritter, *Die Heidelberger Universität. Ein Stück deutscher Geschichte.* Vol. I: *Das Mittelalter (1386-1508).* (Heidelberg: C. Winter, 1936), p. 390.
4. R. Haubst, *Studien zu Nikolaus von Kues und Johannes Wenck* [*Beiträge zur Geschichte der Philosophie des Mittelalters,* 38 (1955)], pp. 99-100.
5. Haubst reasons that *Ap.* 4:21-5:15 sufficiently supports the view that Wenck wrote to the Abbot during the Abbot's lifetime and that the address is not simply a literary device.
6. R. Haubst, *Studien, op. cit..* Cf. p. 103 with p. 84.
7. *Ibid.*, p. 103.
8. *De Ignota Litteratura* will henceforth be abbreviated by "*IL*"; *De Docta Ignorantia* will be abbreviated by "*DI*".
9. E. Vansteenberghe, *Le "De Ignota Litteratura" de Jean Wenck de Herrenberg contre Nicolas de Cuse,* in Vol. 8, Heft 6 (1910) of *Beiträge zur Geschichte der*

Notes to the Introduction

Philosophie des Mittelalters (Münster: Aschendorff, 1912).

10. Vansteenberghe used Codex 190 of the municipal library in Mainz. He did not know of Codex 228/1467 in the Trier municipal library. A. Spamer ["*Zur Überlieferung der Pfeiffer'schen Eckharttexte,*" *Beiträge zur Geschichte der deutschen Sprache und Literatur*, 34 (1909)] had signaled, on pp. 374–375, the presence of this version of *IL*, which he had discovered in 1906. But apparently the librarians at Mainz (whom Vansteenberghe graciously acknowledges in a footnote) did not know of this discovery at Trier either.

A comparison of the two mss. shows that neither is copied from the other. Nor is there sufficient evidence for believing that both were copied from the same third ms. Both appear to be from the middle of the fifteenth century.

11. E.g., Vansteenberghe's edition has "*nostros*" instead of "*nostras*" (20:8); "*vivendum*" instead of "*videndum*" (20:9); "*nocionis*" instead of "*mocionis*, or "*motionis*" (20:13); "*et*" instead of "*in*" (21:9); "*tum*" instead of "*tunc*" (21:30); "*naturali*" instead of "*numerali*" (40:12); "*unitate*" instead of "*veritate*" (40:28), and many, many more such mistakes—not to mention omissions. Moreover, Vansteenberghe alters the words of the ms. without always signaling this fact in his notes. And even though he states in a note on the very first page of his Latin text "*Nous respectons scrupuleusement l'orthographe du Ms.,*" he is far from doing so!

12. In matters that concern textual scholarship (e.g., the preparing of critical editions, the compiling of dictionaries, or the translation of edited texts) I have never yet seen any sizeable work which did not contain errors. Even the most reliable of works—e.g., Klibansky's new text of *DI* III (in the Felix Meiner Latin-German series of Cusa's works)—contain a number of mistakes. In the world of scholarship one scholar can always "score debater's points" against another by finding and parading some such errors of detail. But the fact of scoring such points is impressive only to those readers who are, for better or for worse, among the uninitiate. In the world of scholarship all sins are pardonable—except the sins of carelessness and incompetence. Vansteenberghe's unpardonable sin is not the sin of incompetence.

13. I.e., its clear organization, its smoothness of expression, and its large number of original images and of apt comparisons. See p. 18 of G. Steer, ed., *Johannes Wenck von Herrenberg. Das Büchlein von der Seele* (Munich: W. Fink, 1967).

14. *IL* 31:9–12.
15. *IL* 41:15–16.
16. *IL* 38:11–12.
17. Ps. 45:11 (46:10).
18. *IL* 20:5.
19. *IL* 21:24.
20. *Ap.* 5:6–13; 14:10.

21. "Il y a plus entre l'auteur du 'De Docta Ignorantia' et son adversaire qu'une misérable querelle personnelle, il y a une discussion vraiment et purement philosophique ou théologique. . ." (p. 3 of *Le 'De Ignota Litteratura' de Jean Wenck de Herrenberg*).

22. "Aber zur Erklärung genügt auch frommer Eifer des rechtgläubigen Theologen allein." G. Ritter, *Die Heidelberger Universität, op. cit.* 433.

Notes to the Introduction

23. *Ap.* 5:11–12.

24. "Kurzum, das kirchenpolitische Moment bot Wenck nicht die Waffen, die er zum Kampf benutzte. Trotzdem war gerade dieses die verborgene Triebfeder, ohne die er seine Invektive gegen die Docta ignorantia zumindest nicht so, vielleicht aber überhaubt nicht, geschrieben hätte." *Studien, op. cit.*, p. 113.

25. *Ap.* 23:3.

26. *Ap.* 31:8–9.

27. *IL* is at least as restrained as *Ap*.

28. *Laval théologique et philosophique*, 5 (1949), 213–268. Another prime example would be Mark Fuehrer's "The Principle of *Contractio* in Nicholas of Cusa's Philosophical View of Man," *Downside Review*, 93 (October 1975), 289–296. Fuehrer's mistakes are numerous: (1) He claims that Nicholas teaches that "everything is, in fact, God himself" (290); but this claim is based upon his mistranslation of *DI* I, 22 (69:3–4). (2) He asserts that, for Nicholas, "the creature is primarily a *contractio* of the Maximum" (294); but Nicholas, does not teach that a creature is a *contractio* of God but that he is a contracted reflection of God. (3) According to Fuehrer, "the principle of *contractio* seems to function in Cusa's system in much the same manner as the principle of *methexis* (participation) in Plato's ontology. For Plato, the ontological individual is the entity it happens to be because it participates in its respective universal. Socrates exists as Socrates by participating in the universal 'Socrates'. In Cusa's terminology one would have to say that the individual, Socrates, is the contraction of the universal 'Socrates' " (294). Yet, Plato does not teach that Socrates participates in a universal Socrates; and Fuehrer's claim about the relationship, in Cusa's writings, between the language of participation and the language of contraction is stated too crudely. (4) Fuehrer's point about a creature's having no positivity of its own (291) is based upon his mistranslation and misunderstanding of *DI* II, 2 (103:1–5). This mistranslation is plagiarized from Heron. (6) In presenting Nicholas's example from *DI* II, 2 Fuehrer writes: "There is the face and the image of the face, but no mirror to receive the image of the face" (291). Yet, this assertion is based upon a mistranslation, and it distorts Nicholas's illustration, which is that the mirror is nothing in and of itself *before* and *after* (not during) the appearance of the image; the mirror receives the image but does not exist before receiving it. (7) Fuehrer speaks of the "famous Scholastic dictum, *Quodlibet esse in quolibet*" (292); but this is not a Scholastic dictum and *a fortiori* not a famous one. (8) Fuehrer's closing statement is a gigantic overstatement: "By means of the *via negativa* he [i.e., a human being] thus knows the only truth which Cusa thought worth knowing: that the Absolute is the infinite" (296). (9) All of Fuehrer's references are to the Basel edition (1565) of the Latin text of *DI*, rather than to the critical edition published by the Heidelberg Academy. Thus, the reader is left to figure out whether or not these two texts have the same readings for the passages cited by Fuehrer. Moreover, since none of Fuehrer's references indicate the Book and Chapter of *DI*, but indicate only the page number in the Basel edition, the reader is forced to consult the outdated, and not easily accessible, Basel edition in order to locate a passage in the critical edition or in any translation. (10) Fuehrer's article neither explicitly takes account of, nor mentions, previously published articles on Cusa (except for Duclow's); several of these are crucial for his topic. Indeed, a number of striking points already made in the literature are reduplicated in Fuehrer's article.

Notes to the Introduction

It is time for editors of scholarly journals to insist once more upon scholarly standards—such as the use of critical editions of texts, the citing of published translations which are being followed, and the listing of important previously published articles on the topic being addressed. One wonders, for instance, about an interpretation of Spinoza's "ontological" argument, appearing in the *Philosophical Review* in 1979, in which no edition of the Latin text of Spinoza's *Ethics* is named, no Latin passages are ever presented, no indication is given of the translation on which the interpretation of the arguments is based, and no full translation of the disputed passages is ever presented.

29. Martin's text has "or," which is presumably a misprint for "of".
30. Martin, 224.
31. By contrast, Martin claims: "To say that God is *omnium complicatio* is completely different from saying that He possesses eminently the perfection of any possible creature. It means, quite definitely, that He is conceived in terms of composition, even though real composition is at the same time denied. Cusa evades this contradiction by attributing it to reason" (232). Cf. *Ap.* 27:2–6: "We know from the Apostle Paul and from all the wise that God is in all things and that all things are in Him. However, no one [who holds this position] thereby affirms that there is composition in God; for in God all things are God. For example, in God the earth is not the earth but is God—and similarly regarding each other thing. Hence, when that man infers that this [doctrine] is inconsistent with the [doctrine of] divine simplicity, he understands nothing at all."
32. *Ap.* 17:4–6.
33. Martin, 216.
34. *DI* III, 1 (184:7–15; 185:3–9).
35. That Nicholas believes there to be unactualized creatable things is obvious from *DI* I, 22. Cf. *DP* 8:11–13. Martin, on p. 219, grants this point of interpretation; but he does not realize that his doing so is inconsistent with his use of the word "mere" in the sentence now being discussed.

In *DI* II, 8 Nicholas writes: "Although God is infinite and therefore had the power to create the world as infinite, nevertheless because the possibility was, necessarily, contracted and was not at all absolute or infinite aptitude, the world—in accordance with the possibility of being—was not able to be actually infinite or greater or to exist in any other way [than it does]"(139:1–5). Nicholas's word "greater" is—here as elsewhere—vague. Let us note here only the following point: though Nicholas maintains that this world, i.e., our world, could not have been "greater" than it is, he also maintains that a greater world than this world could have been created (though an actually infinite world could not have been created). See the references given in n. 35 of the notes to Book Three.

36. Martin, 216.
37. Martin, 219.
38. *DI* II, 8 (140:7–8); II, 4 (114:2–4). Also note *De Coniecturis* I, 5 (18:1–2) and *De Pace Fidei* 12 (36:6–9).
39. *DI* II, 9 (150:9–10).
40. *DI* II, 3 (111:3–4).
41. Martin, 216.
42. *Ap.* 31:8–9. Nicholas, of course, does speak as follows in *DI* III, 1 (185:1–3):

Notes to the Introduction

"There is only one Limit of species, of genera, or of the universe. This Limit is the Center, the Circumference, and the Union of all things." But God is the Limit of all things in the sense that He is the Absolute Maximum, which is actually all that which can be. He is not a Limit toward which the creation converges.

43. Martin, 248.
44. Martin, 248.
45. *DI* II, 8 (136:7–8).
46. *DI* II, 8 (137:1–2 and 11–12).
47. *DI* II, 1 (97:7–8).
48. When we compare *DI* II, 8, *Idiota de Mente* 7 (the title and 107:4-14), and *DP* 6-8, we see more clearly that Nicholas uses "*possibilitas absoluta*" in two senses, depending on the context. In one sense it refers to God, who is also eternal actuality. In another sense it refers to altogether unformed matter (which Aristotle called prime matter)—i.e., to pure matter, matter apart from all form. Through negation we can speak meaningfully of unformed matter, teaches Nicholas; but unformed matter does not exist, is not actual. Hence, it is not God, who does exist, who is Actualized-possibility.
49. Martin, 234.
50. *Ap*. 26:11-12 and 18-19. Also note *De Visione Dei* 9 (36:10-12); 14 (63:1-10). *De Ludo Globi* 2 (91:10 - 92:1).
51. *DI* III, 1 (186:7).
52. Martin, 267.
53. Moreover, although Nicholas teaches that the whole of the creation is contingent, he denies that the relation between the Creator and the creation can be understood in terms of the relation between substance and accident [*DI* II, 3 (110:12–25)]. Nor does he anywhere explicitly call the creation an accident of the one divine Essence.
54. *Ap*. 33:20–25.
55. Martin might have strengthened the *appearance* of his case if he had taken account of certain expressions in *De Dato Patris Luminum*. The present Introduction does not permit a discussion of these passages at this time. But I deal with them in detail in my book *Nicholas of Cusa's Metaphysic of Contraction*, in which I also present a translation of *De Dato Patris Luminum*.
56. Martin, 256–257.
57. Martin, 258.
58. *DI* II, 8 (140:7–8).
59. *DI* II, 2 (103:3–4).
60. Martin, 216.
61. *IL* 36:30–31.
62. *DI* I, 11 (30:14–17). In *Ap*. Nicholas himself does not always quote *DI* exactly. E.g., *Ap*. 30:14 has "*ipsum maximum*", though *DI* I, 11 (30:13) has "*ipsum unum*". And though the letter to Cardinal Julian [*DI* III (263:9)] has "*incorruptibilium*", *Ap*. 11:6 has "*corruptibilium*".
63. See n. 209 of the notes to *Unknown Learning*.
64. See n. 13 of the notes to *Ap*.
65. He wrote: "*visus. N.*" The *explicit* of the Trier ms. (Codex Trevir. Latinus 1926) also states that the work is Nicholas's.

Notes to the Introduction

66. Also note *Ap.* 9:6.
67. Josef Koch, *Die Ars coniecturalis des Nikolaus von Kues* (Cologne: Westdeutscher Verlag, 1956), p. 16. (Heft 16 of *Arbeitsgemeinschaft für Forschung des Landes Nordrhein-Westfalen.*)
68. See his discussion of thesis two, as well as *IL* 23:26–24:7.
69. *Ap.* 18:26–19:10.
70. *Ap.* 4:20–21.
71. *Ap.* 25:9.
72. See Edmond Vansteenberghe, *Autour de la Docte Ignorance. Une controverse sur la Théologie mystique au XVe siècle [Beiträge zur Geschichte der Philosophie des Mittelalters*, 14 (1915)].
73. *DI* II, 2 (101:3–4). *DP* 12:1–3.
74. *DI* I, 8 (22:7–8).
75. *DI* II, 2 (104:6).
76. *DI* II, 2 (100:12–14). Cf. II, 13 (180:1–13). Note I, 1 (2:11–15): "Wherefore, we say that a sound, free intellect knows to be true what it insatiably desires to attain (while it surveys all things by means of its innate faculty of inference) and what is apprehended by its affectionate embrace. That from which no sound mind can withhold assent is, we have no doubt, most true." Nicholas does not deny that we have knowledge of various basic principles or even of material objects. But "the precise combinations in corporeal things and the congruent relating of known to unknown surpass human reason . . ." (4:1–3).

NOTES TO *UNKNOWN LEARNING*

1. This work was composed sometime during 1442–1443. See Rudolf Haubst, *Studien zu Nikolaus von Kues und Johannes Wenck [Beiträge zur Geschichte der Philosophie des Mittelalters*, 38 (1955)], p. 99.
2. John of Gelnhausen was a member of the Council of Basel, as was John Wenck.
3. Ps. 70:16 (71:16). The Douay and the King James versions are quite different here.
4. Rom. 10:3.
5. Luke 10:35.
6. Ecclesiasticus 24:31.
7. Ps. 45:11 (46:10).
8. Ps. 45:10 (46:9).
9. Matt. 20:6.
10. Rom. 1:21.
11. Wenck's text has "*humanitus*", Nicholas's "*humaniter*".
12. See Nicholas's *Letter to Cardinal Julian* [*DI* III (263:7–9)].
13. I John 4:1.
14. II Cor. 11:13.
15. Mark 1:15.
16. John 10:35.
17. Gal. 1:8.
18. I Cor. 13:12.
19. Boethius's *De Consolatione Philosophiae* V,4 has "Omne enim quod cognoscitur non secundum sui uim sed secundum cognoscentium potius comprehenditur facultatem" (H.F. Stewart-E.K. Rand edition). N.B. Aquinas, *Summa Theologiae* Ia, 75, 5. Cf. *Liber de Causis*, end of section 9 (p. 174 of Bardenhewer's edition, cited fully in n. 135 below).
20. Aristotle, *De Anima* III, 2 (425^b19–26).
21. *Letter to Cardinal Julian* [*DI* III (264:1-3)].
22. Aristotle, *Metaphysics* IV, 4 (1006^b19f.). Cf. IV, 3 (1005^b19–20).
23. This sentence and the previous one are cited from *Letter to Cardinal Julian* [*DI* III (264:4–9)]. Wenck writes "*incrementum*", but the better mss. of Nicholas's text have "*crementum*".
24. *DI* I, 10 (27:11–15).

Notes to Unknown Learning

25. *DI* I, Prologue (1:19–23).
26. Aristotle, *Metaphysics*, opening sentence.
27. *Ibid.*, I, 2 (982^{b}12–14).
28. *DI* I, 1 (2:3–9).
29. See n. 6 of the notes to Book One of *DI*, in my *Nicholas of Cusa on Learned Ignorance*.
30. *DI* I, 1 (2:16–17).
31. See Aristotle, *Metaphysics* I, 9 (992^{b}31–32).
32. These two sentences are a paraphrase of *DI* I, 1 (2:17–21).
33. Isa. 29:12. Cf. verse 11.
34. Ps. 70:15–16 (71:15–16). See the comment in n. 3 above.
35. Isa. 29:14.
36. Isa. 29:15.
37. Eph. 5:8.
38. Rom. 10:2.
39. See the title of *DI* I, 1.
40. *DI* I, 17 (51:7–9).
41. *DI* I, 1 (3:2–6); II, 2 (102:4–5).
42. *DI* I, 4 (11:7–9). Cf. I, 3 (9:5–7).
43. Cf. *DI* I, 12 (33:14–15).
44. *DI* I, 13 (33:16). Cf. the title of *DI* I, 4.
45. *DI* I, 2 (8:5–7).
46. *DI* I, 4 (11:4–7).
47. Wisd. 13:5.
48. Ps. 91:5 (92:4).
49. Ps. 150:1 (150:1).

50. A *conclusio* is a thesis which has a *probatio* (supporting reason) and, possibly, a *correlarium*. The *probatio* usually begins with the word "*patet*". In Wenck's citations from Nicholas's text I have italicized the words "this is evident," even though "*patet*" is Wenck's word more than it is Nicholas's.

51. Nicholas nowhere says this. In *Ap*. he repudiates it. But note such passages as *DI* I, 4 (12:4–7), which undoubtedly confused Wenck.

52. *DI* I, 4 (11:7–8; 12:12).
53. *DI* I, 2 (5:8,11).

54. *DI* I, 24 (74:10–75:2), where Nicholas alludes to Pseudo-Hermes Trismegistus's *Asclepius* 20 [*Corpus Hermeticum*, Vol. 2 (Paris: Société d'Edition "Les Belles Lettres," 1945), p. 321, especially lines 7–9 of the Latin text, ed. A. D. Nock]. Also note Proposition 13 of his *Book of Twenty-four Philosophers* [Clemens Baeumker, ed., "Das pseudo-hermetische 'Buch der vierundzwanzig Meister' (Liber XXIV philosophorum). Ein Beitrag zur Geschichte des Neupythagoreismus und Neuplatonismus im Mittelalter," in *Beiträge zur Geschichte der Philosophie und Theologie des Mittelalters*, 25 (1928), 194–214].

55. *DI* I, 24 (75:2–5; 74:8–12).

56. *Das Buch der göttlichen Tröstung*, written either (as Wenck believes) for Elsbeth, wife of King Albert of Hungary, or for Agnes, their daughter. The Latin words

Notes to Unknown Learning

with which the work begins are taken from II Cor. 1:3. For the German text see *Meister Eckharts Buch der göttlichen Tröstung und von dem edlen Menschen (liber Benedictus)*, ed. Philipp Strauch [in *Kleine Texte für theologische und philologische Vorlesungen und Übungen*, ed. Hans Lietzmann (Bonn: A. Marcus and E. Weber's, 1910), No. 55]. For an English version see "The Book of Comfort" in *Meister Eckhart: A Modern Translation*, trans. Raymond B. Blakney (New York: Harper and Row Torchbooks, 1941), pp. 43–73.

57. *Ibid.*, p. 9, lines 14–19 (English translation, pp. 45–46).

58. *Eine lateinische Rechtfertigungsschrift des Meister Eckhart*, ed. A. Daniels [*Beiträge zur Geschichte der Philosophie des Mittelalters*, 23 (1923)], p. 33, lines 27–37. See Meister Eckhart. *Die deutschen Werke*, Vol. I: *Meister Eckharts Predigten*. Ed. and trans. Josef Quint (Stuttgart: W. Kohlhammer, 1958). Sermon 2: "*Intravit Jesus in quoddam castellum, etc.*" (Luke 10:38), section 5, pp. 44–45 (= *Meister Eckhart: A Modern Translation*, *op. cit.*, p. 211).

59. Wenck's text has "*maximitate absoluta*" (26:1–2). Nicholas's recapitulation has "*in maximitate absoluta*" (*Ap.* 25:14).

60. *DI* I, 2 (6:1–2); I, 6 (15: 12–13, 17–18).

61. See Meister Eckhart. *Die lateinischen Werke*, Vol. I: *Prologi. Expositio Libri Genesis. Liber Parabolarum Genesis. Ed. and trans.* Konrad Weiss *(Stuttgart: W. Kohlhammer, 1964)*, p. 38 [*Prologus Generalis*].

62. *Ibid.*, p. 50 [*Expositio libri Genesis*, cap. 1, v. 1].

63. Wisd. 11:21–23. Where I have used ellipses, Wenck has inserted the parenthetical clause: "'*antelucanus*' is a single word which means 'before existing light'; for *lucanus* is the morning brightness."

64. Heb. 1:3.

65. *DI* I, 2 (6:6–8).

66. *DI* II 10 (153:1–4), to which Wenck is alluding, has "enfolding" ("*complicatio*") instead of "unfolding" ("*explicatio*"). See the comment in n. 97 below.

67. *DI* I, 1 (2:16–17; 3:2–3); I, 3 (title). Cf. Aristotle, *Physics* I, 4 (187^{b}9–13).

68. See *DI* I, 17 (51: 7–9) and I, 4 (title). By "earlier" Wenck indicates that he has earlier alluded to these passages. See n. 40 and n. 44 above.

69. Peter Lombard's *Sentences*, Book I, Distinctio 3 (*PL* 192:529–530).

70. *DI* I, 3 (9:14–15).

71. *DI* I, 3 (9:10–13; 10:9–13).

72. Aristotle, *Categories* 6 (6^{a}28–36); 8 (11^{a}17–18).

73. Aristotle, *De Caelo*. Cf. I, 6 (274^{a}19.2); I, 7 (275^{b}22–24); I, 12 (283^{a}7–9.1).

74. Cf. Boethius, *Commentaria in Porphyrium a se translatum* (*PL* 64:101–102).

75. See Aristotle's *Metaphysics* X, 4-5 (e.g., 1055^{a}4.2 & 1056^{a}14.2), not *Physics* I.

76. For the list and location of Wenck's unpublished mss. see Klaus D. Kuhnekath, *Die Philosophie des Johannes Wenck von Herrenberg im Vergleich zu den Lehren des Nikolaus von Kues* (Cologne: University of Cologne Ph.D. dissertation 1975).

77. *DI* I, 3 (10:1–2; 9:16–17).

78. See, e.g., *De Anima* III, 7 (431^{a}17–18) and III, 4 (429^{a}15–18).

79. *DI* I, 3 (10:18–19).

80. *DI* I, 3 (10:6–8).

Notes to Unknown Learning

81. Two paragraphs earlier.
82. Aristotle, *De Anima* III, 4 (429ª27–30).
83. At 21:9 Wenck cites I Cor. 13:12, a verse which indicates that a purer knowledge is reserved for the future state. See also 24:9-10 and 27:20-23.
84. See the first corollary of thesis four. Also see Wenck's citation at 23:26–24:2.
85. Aristotle, *De Anima* III, 4 (429ª15–17).
86. Aristotle, *Posterior Analytics* I, 2 (71ᵇ9.1–15, 30–32).
87. *DI* I, 4 (12:18–25).
88. *DI* I, 4 (11:13–15; 12:1–5).
89. At the beginning of *IL* 22. See n. 22 above.
90. *DI* I, 4 (12:7–8).
91. *DI* I, 4 (12:10–11).
92. *DI* I, 11 (30:7–17). Wenck's words ". . . *cum similitudo exemplaris sit hoc ipsum quod exemplar in unitate naturae*" misconstrue Nicholas's text. Wenck fails to recognize that Nicholas's expression "Maximal Image" refers not to the universe (which Nicholas calls a *maximum* and which he alludes to at the outset of *DI* I, 11) but to the Son of God, who is the Image of the Father, according to Scripture (Col. 1:15).
93. Meister Eckhart. *Die deutschen Werke.* Vol. I: *Meister Eckharts Predigten.* Ed. and trans. Josef Quint (Stuttgart: W. Kohlhammer, 1958). Sermon 6: "*Iusti vivent in aeternum*" (Wisd. 5:16), pp. 109–110 (= *Meister Eckhart: A Modern Translation, op. cit.*, p. 181).
94. *DI* I, 12 (33:6–7).
95. *DI* I, 12 (33:4–6). Regarding the inference that God is undifferentiated and precise, see such passages as I, 4 (12:4–7); I, 16 (45: 16–17).
96. I John 3:2.
97. Wenck writes: "*Nostra ignorantia incomprehensibiliter docebit . . . .*" But *DI* I, 12 (33:16) has: ". . . *nostra ignorantia incomprehensibiliter docebitur. . . .*" This miscontrual is so gross as to suggest that Wenck is working with a copy of *DI* which is here inaccurate.
98. *DI* I, 12 (33:16–18).
99. *DI*, I, 12 (33:14–15). Wenck here betrays a total misunderstanding of Nicholas's text. See n. 97 above.
100. Here, as at 34:2, Wenck uses "*doctrina*" and "*scientia*" interchangeably.
101. *DI* I, 1 (4:3–4; 2:16–18).
102. I Cor. 2:2.
103. Isa. 29:11–12. Cf. Wenck's use of these verses in discussing his title (*IL* 23:10).
104. Ecclesiastes 1:18.
105. Ecclesiasticus 24:29.
106. Aristotle, *Physics* I, 9 (192ª17–19).
107. "*Abgescheiden leben.*" See Eduard Schaefer, *Meister Eckeharts Traktat "von Abegescheidenheit." Untersuchung und Textneuausgabe* [Bonn: Ludwig Röhrscheid, 1955 (Ph.D. dissertation, University of Saarland)]. Also see *Meister Eckhart: A Modern Translation, op. cit.*, pp. 82–91. At *Ap.*31:15 Nicholas replaces "*abgescheiden leben*" by "*abstracta vita*".

Notes to Unknown Learning

108. Ps. 45:11 (46:10).
109. *Ibid.*
110. *DI* I, 16 (42:8–10).
111. *DI* I, 16 (42:11–14).
112. *DI* I, 16 (43:6–7).
113. Aristotle, *Physics* I, 2 (185ª12–13).
114. Ps. 45:11 (46:10).
115. See the reference given in n. 23 above.
116. John 5:39.
117. I Pet 2:2.
118. Matt. 22:29.
119. Gal. 5:20.
120. I Cor. 1:25.
121. John 1:45.
122. *DI* I, 16 (43:13–16).
123. *DI* I, 17 (51:7–8). Cf. I, 23 (73:3).
124. John 1:3.
125. *DI* I, 16 (44:7–8). Nicholas is citing Moses Maimonides' view, with which he here agrees.
126. Wenck seems to have invented this *probatio*.
127. *DI* I, 16 (46:10–12).
128. *DI* I, 16 (46:12–13).
129. Aristotle, *Metaphysics* X, 1 (1052ᵇ19.1–2, 34–37). Cf. *DI* I, 17 (47:12–14).
130. *DI* I, 19 (57:11–20).
131. *DI* I, 19 (57:16–17, 21).
132. *DI* I 23 (71:1–3).
133. See n. 100 above.
134. Ecclesiasticus 36:27.
135. *Liber de Causis*, section 19. [*Die pseudo-aristotelische Schrift Ueber das reine Gute bekannt unter dem Namen Liber de causis*, ed. Otto Bardenhewer (Freiburg: Herder'sche Verlagshandlung, 1882), p. 181, lines 7–8. Reprinted Frankfurt: Minerva GmbH, n.d.]
136. *DI* I, 19 (58:3–4). Wenck's text reads "*anguli aut trianguli*", though Nicholas writes "*anguli trianguli*". Wenck's extract is garbled; for according to Nicholas's account, the angles are in the maximum triangle, not in the unqualifiedly Maximum. Wenck here confuses Nicholas's mathematical illustration with the claims about the unqualifiedly Maximum.
137. *DI* I, 19 (58:4–5, 6–8); I, 16 (43:3–4).
138. Heb. 13:9.
139. *DI* I, 21 (63:10–11).
140. DI I, 21 (63:11–14).
141. *DI* I, 26 (87:7–11).
142. *DI* I, 22 (67:6–9; 69:1–3).
143. *DI* I, 22 (69:3–4, 7, 10–11).
144. *DI* I, 24 (75:4–10).

Notes to Unknown Learning

145. *DI* II, 3 (106:1–5).
146. *DI* I, 24 (80:17–18).
147. Aristotle, *De Interpretatione* 9 (19ª29.3–32).
148. *DI* II, 2 (101:12–13, 6–7).
149. *DI* II, 2 (102:1–2).
150. *DI* II, 3 (107:1).
151. *DI* II, 3 (107:11–12).
152. *DI* II, 3 (108: 1–2; 107:6; 106:11–12).
153. Ps. 15:2 (16:2).
154. Ecclesiastes 1:7.
155. *DI* II, 3 (110:11–12).
156. *DI* II, 3 (110:12–13).
157. Cf. *DI* II, 3 (110:12–13) with II, 3 (111:15–22).
158. I.e., to-be-in-no-respect is to-be-nothing.
159. *DI* II, 4 (115:5–6).
160. *DI* II, 4 (115:6–7).
161. *DI* II, 4 (115:13–14).
162. *DI* II, 4 (115:16–17; 116:21).
163. *DI* II, 5 (118: 15–17).
164. *DI* II, 5 (118:14–15).
165. *DI* II, 4 (115:17–19).
166. *DI* II, 9 (143:6–7). Nicholas attributes this view to the Platonists. Wenck has no good reason for believing that Nicholas endorses it.
167. *DI* II, 9 (143:7–8).
168. *DI* II, 9 (145:13–14).
169. I.e., all motions, which are the unfolding of rest. *DI* II, 10 (155:3–4). II, 3 (106:2–3).
170. I.e., as a circle is the unfolding of a center. *DI* II, 9 (145:14).
171. Aristotle. *Physics* VIII, 10 (267ª22–267ᵇ2).
172. *DI* II, 11 (157:23–26). Cusa's text reads: "*Qui est simul omnium circumferentia infinita.*"
173. *DI* II, 11 (157:22–23).
174. *DI* II, 12 (166:1; 167:8–9).
175. *DI* II, 13, (177:10–17).
176. *DI* II, 13 (177:11). I John 1:5.
177. *DI* III, 2 (190:9–13).
178. *DI* III, 2 (191:1–3).
179. *DI* III, 2 (192:6–7; 191:13–14).
180. Aristotle, *Metaphysics* IX. E.g., IX, 3 (1047ª19f.).
181. *DI* III, 2 (191:8–11; 194:5–6).
182. *DI* III, 2 (193:2–3).
183. *DI* III, 9 (233:11–12).
184. *DI* III, 9 (233:12–13, 17–18).
185. Rev. 3:17–18.
186. John 1:14. See Augustine *On the Gospel of John* 2.16 (*PL* 35:1395).

Notes to Unknown Learning

187. *DI* III, 4 (204:20–22). Whereas Wenck's text has "*cum humanitate Ihesu maximi*", Nicholas's has "*cum humanitate Jesu maxima*".
188. This summary of the *probatio* distorts Nicholas's reasoning. *DI* III, 4 (204:13–19, 22–23).
189. *DI* III, 6 (219:2–8).
190. *DI* III, 6 (219:10–14).
191. Cf. Rom. 5:10; Phil. 3:18.
192. Ps. 70:15–16 (71:15–16). See the comment in n. 3 above.
193. I Cor. 6:17.
194. *DI* III, 7 (225:13–14).
195. *DI* III 7 (225:20–21; 226:2–4, 8–13).
196. Gal. 4:4.
197. I.e., denies that Christ had a real body.
198. *DI* III, 8 (227:15–16).
199. *DI* III, 8 (227:12–13, 17–22).
200. I.e., to be more than one person, each having one and the same nature.
201. *DI* III, 12 (260: 12–14).
202. *DI* III, 12 (261:1–3).
203. *DI* III, 12 (262:4–7).
204. *DI* III, 12 (257:9–10).
205. *DI* III, 12 (254:20–22).
206. *Letter to Cardinal Julian* [*DI* III (264:7–9)].
207. James 3:6.
208. II Cor. 11:3, 13.
209. The *explicit* reads: "And this is the end to what was written cursorily at Heidelberg." I opt for the transcription "*cursorie*" (rather than "*cursoriae*"); and I take it to mean "cursorily" rather than to be an allusion to the cursory lessons at the University of Heidelberg. Cf. Nicholas of Cusa, *Idiota de Mente* 7 (106:15-16): "*Haec autem nunc sic dixerim cursorie et rustice.*" Cf. ibid., 15 (160:1): "*Haec sic cursim dicta ab idiota grate recipito.*"

NOTES TO *A DEFENSE OF LEARNED IGNORANCE*

1. Viz., Cardinal Julian Cesarini (1398–1444). See n. 1 of *DI* Notes to Book One.
2. I John 1:5.
3. Philo, *Questions and Answers on Genesis* IV, 191. Trans. Ralph Marcus [Cambridge, Mass.: Harvard University Press, 1953 (Loeb Library Series, Supplementary Vol. I)]. Also see Gen. 26:15.
4. Matt. 13:44.
5. *Unknown Learning* is addressed to John of Gelnhausen, once abbot of Maulbronn.
6. *IL* 41:15. In *Ap.* Wenck is referred to throughout as "the Adversary," Nicholas as "the Teacher.". The term "*adversarius*" may well have been chosen with an eye to I Pet.. 5:8.
7. Hermes Trismegistus, *Asclepius* 1 [*Corpus Hermeticum*, ed. A. D. Nock (Paris: Société d'Edition "Les Belles Lettres," Vol. 2, 1945), p. 297, lines 8–9]. Pseudo-Dionysius, *The Divine Names I*, 8 [*Dionysiaca* I, 56 (Paris: Desclée de Brouwer, 2 vols., 1937, 1950)].
8. Matt. 7:6.
9. II Cor. 12:2–4.
10. Pseudo-Dionysius, *The Divine Names* VIII, 6 (*Dionysiaca* I, 428–432). N. B. The divisions in the Latin translation by Ambrose Traversari differ from the standard ones. Nicholas uses Ambrose's translation.
11. II Tim. 2:13. Nicholas writes "*ignorare*", though both the Vulgate and the Latin translations in *Dionysiaca* I, 429 have "*negare*".
12. Ps. 45:11 (46:10). Cited from Wenck's text (19:22–23).
13. The clause "God wills to remove our leisure" misrepresents Wenck's text.
14. *IL* 20:7–17.
15. *IL* 20:17–20.
16. Plato, *Apology* 31d. Apuleius, *De Deo Socratis* 6.133 [p. 26 of Apulée, *Opuscules philosophiques et fragments*, ed. and trans. Jean Beaujeu (Paris: Société d'Edition "Les Belles Lettres," 1973)]. Philo, *Questions and Answers on Genesis, op. cit.*, IV, 188.
17. This is the description formulated by Anselm of Canterbury in *Proslogion* 2. It may have been suggested to Anselm by certain closely similar descriptions in Augustine: e.g., *Confessions* VII, 4: "*Neque enim ulla anima unquam potuit poteritve cogitare aliquid quod sit te melius, qui summum et optimum bonum es*" (*PL* 32:735).

Notes to A Defense of Learned Ignorance

18. Nicholas here refers to God as "*this* Form," though a few lines earlier he stated that God "is not this or that." These statements are not incompatible. In the present sentence and the subsequent ones "this Form" is a place holder for "Form of forms," "Absolute Form." Absolute Form is not this or that form (e.g., form of the sky, form of the earth, etc.).

19. *Metaphysica*, Tractate X, chap. 2 (Venice edition of 1498).

20. *Ibid.*

21. Pseudo-Dionysius, *The Divine Names* VII, 1 (*Dionysiaca* I, 385–386.)

22. *IL* 20:21–26.

23. Both *IL* and Nicholas's letter [*DI* III (263:9)] have "*incorruptibilium*".

24. *IL* 21:8–11.

25. Pseudo-Dionysius, *Epistola* 1: "To Gaius" (*Dionysiaca* I, 607). Cf. *DP* 53:14.

26. Augustine, Sermon 117, chap. 3 (*PL* 38:663).

27. Algazel, *Philosophia*, Book I, Tractatus III (the very end) [*Logica et Philosophia Algazelis Arabis*, edition of Peter Liechtensteyn (Venice, 1506)].

28. Augustine, *Epistola* 130 ("To Proba"), chaps. 14–15 (*PL* 33:505).

29. *Ibid.*, chap. 15 (*PL* 33:505–506) N.B. Add as note for 13:16 of Klibansky's text of *Ap*.: 'dicat: dicit *Tr*'.

30. Acts 17:27.

31. *De Quaerendo Deum* I (18:2–5) [Vol. 4 of *Opera Omnia* (Hamburg: Felix Meiner, 1959)].

32. *IL* 21:20–24.

33. *IL* 21:34–22:1.

34. John 3:32. II Cor. 12:2–4.

35. Rom. 10:17.

36. In the corresponding line of the Latin text (*Ap*. 14:22) I am reading "*aliquid*" for "*aliud*". This is a conjecture.

37. Jerome, *De Viris Inlustribus*, chap. 11 [ed. Guilelmus Herdingius (Leipzig: B. G. Teubner, 1879), p. 17].

38. Algazel, *Logica, op. cit.*, chap. 1.

39. *De Coniecturis* I, 6 (25:10–17); II, 1 (76–78).

40. In *De Coniecturis* II, 1 (78:13–15) Nicholas states that in God all things coincide without any difference. But he nowhere therein explicitly states that God is beyond the coincidence of contradictories, as he does at the end of *De Visione Dei* 9.

41. Pseudo-Dionysius, *The Divine Names* V, 10 [*Dionysiaca* I, 364 (last line) and 365 (first line) of Ambrose's translation].

42. Henry Bate of Mechlin, *Speculum divinorum et quorundam naturalium*, ed. G. Wallerand (Louvain, 1931). [R. Klibansky, ed., *Ap*., p. 15n.: The passage envisioned by Nicholas is nowhere to be found. But II, 36–37 and II, 21 (p. 226 and pp. 190–191 of Wallerand) come closest to it.]

43. Augustine, *Confessions* XIII, 37 (PL 32:868).

44. Note Wenck's first thesis, which is discussed later in *Ap*. The present allusion seems to be to Wenck's exordium. (See *Ap*. 7:10–22.)

45. I Cor. 2:14. This verse is alluded to in *DI* III, 6 (216:2–3).

Notes to A Defense of Learned Ignorance

46. R. Klibansky, ed., *Ap.*, p. 16n., refers the reader to acts 6 and 14 of the sixth ecumenical council (680/681). [J. D. Mansi, *Sacrorum conciliorum nova et amplissima collectio*, 31 vols. (Venice, 1757–1798), Vol. 11 (1765), pp. 326, 595. Reprinted and continued in 60 vols., ed. L. Petit and J. B. Martin (Paris, 1899–1927)].

47. *De Dato Patris Luminum* III (105) [Vol. 4 of *Opera Omnia* (Hamburg: Felix Meiner, 1959)].

48. St. Thomas, *Summa Contra Gentiles* I, 26.

49. Pseudo-Dionysius, *The Celestial Hierarchy* IV, 1 (*Dionysiaca* II, 802).

50. Pseudo-Dionysius, *The Divine Names* I, 5 (*Dionysiaca* I, 39).

51. *DI* I, 5 (13:22–29).

52. Viz., the assumption that Nicholas regards Creator and creature as coinciding. See *Ap.* 16:10–11.

53. *IL* 23:23–24.

54. Pseudo-Dionysius, *The Divine Names* I, 1 (*Dionysiaca* I, 7).

55. The Latin translation by Ambrose Traversari has the word "*noscitur*"; nonetheless, Nicholas says "*nescitur*". See *Dionysiaca* I, 8.

56. Pseudo-Dionysius, *The Divine Names* I, 1 (*Dionysiaca* I, 7–8).

57. *IL* 23:35–24:2.

58. Wisd. 13:5.

59. This is implied in *IL* 24:2–9.

60. *IL* 24:7–16.

61. Nicholas says "*repperisse*", whereas both mss. of Wenck's treatise have "*recepisse*".

62. The feast day of Dionysius is Oct. 9.

63. Pseudo-Dionysius, *The Mystical Theology* I, 3 (*Dionysiaca* I, 577).

64. Maximus the Confessor, in his various commentaries on Dionysius. The exact sentence alluded to by Nicholas seems nowhere to be found. The passage agrees more closely with Thierry of Chartres, *Commentarius in Librum Boetii de Trinitate* (*PL* 95:398).

65. Pseudo-Dionysius, *The Mystical Theology* I, 3 (*Dionysiaca* I, 575).

66. *Ibid.*, I, 1 (*Dionysiaca* I, 568).

67. *Ibid.*, I, 2 (*Dionysiaca* I, 569–570).

68. *Ibid.*, I, 2 (*Dionysiaca* I, 569).

69. I.e., Robert Grosseteste.

70. I.e., Thomas Gallus.

71. Found in Henricus Cornelius Agrippa of Nettesheim, *Apologia adversus calumnias propter declamationem de vanitate scientiarum et excellentia verbi Dei, sibi per aliquos Lovanienses theologistas intentatas* [in Vol. II of the *Opera in duos tomos* (Lyons, n.d.), section 9 (p. 286)].

72. Viz., the untruth that logic provides a precise comparative relation to God. See *Ap.* 19:18–22.

73. *IL* 24:17–26.

74. See n. 56 of the English translation of *IL*.

75. *IL* 25:17–21.

76. *IL* 25:22–32.

Notes to A Defense of Learned Ignorance

77. *DI* II, 2 (100:3–4).
78. *DI* I, 21 (66:4–8).
79. *DI* I, 19.
80. R. Klibansky, ed., *A.*, p. 23n.: "This statement is not found in Celestine I or in the other popes with this name."
81. R. Klibansky, ed., *Ap.*, p. 24n.: "Augustine's works . . . nowhere exhibit these words"; but the meaning corresponds to *De Trinitate* VI, 7 (*PL* 42:929); VI, 10 (*PL* 42:932); VIII, 1 (*PL* 42:947).
82. Note Thierry of Chartres, *Commentarius in Librum Boetii de Trinitate* (*PL* 95:404).
83. See the Athansian Creed.
84. *DI* I, 24.
85. R. Klibansky, ed., *Ap.*, p. 25n.: "John Guldenschaf [was] dean of the clergy of St. Stephan's at Mainz from 1436 until his death in 1439."
86. A. Daniels, *Eine lateinische Rechtfertigungsschrift des Meister Eckhart* [in *Beiträge zur Geschichte der Philosophie des Mittelalters*, 23 (1923)].
87. *IL* does not have the Latin word *"in"*.
88. *IL* 26:1–3.
89. *IL* 26:3–5.
90. *IL* 26:20–21.
91. Augustine, *Confessions* I, 6. Nicholas takes this quotation from Meister Eckhart. See Meister Eckhart, *Die lateinischen Werke*, Vol. I: *Prologi. Expositio Libri Genesis. Liber Parabolarum Genesis.* Ed. and trans. Konrad Weiss (Stuttgart: W. Kohlhammer, 1964), p. 46.
92. Gen. 2:7,
93. Cf. *Ap.* 27:4–5.
94. Meister Eckhart, *Prologi, op. cit.*, p.45.
95. *IL* 26:27–28.
96. *IL* 26:31–33.
97. Rom. 11:36. Col. 1:16.
98. *IL* 26:35–27:1.
99. *IL* 27:4–5.
100. *IL* :8–12.
101. Corollary 1 of thesis 2 (*IL* 27:29–31).
102. *IL* 28:8–10.
103. Corollary 2 of thesis 2 (*IL* 28:13–15).
104. *IL* 28:26–27.
105. *IL* 29:15–19.
106. *Ap.* 15.
107. Pseudo-Dionysius, *The Divine Names* I, 7 (*Dionysiaca* I, 48–51).
108. *IL* 29:32–34.
109. John Andrea, *Novella super primo libro decretalium* [heading "De Summa Trinitate et Fide Catholica"; section "Damnamus" (Vol. I, p.5 verso, col. 2)]. Venice, 1489.
110. II Cor. 3:6.
111. *IL* 30:8–9. Cf. 30:10–12.

Notes to A Defense of Learned Ignorance

112. *Ap.* has *"ipsum maximum"*, whereas *DI* has *"ipsum unum"*.
113. Col. 1:15. Heb. 1:3.
114. *IL* 31:7–8, 13–16.
115. Nicholas uses the Latin *"abstracta vita"* for Wenck's German phrase *"abgescheiden leben"*. See *IL* 31:24.
116. *IL* 31:29–31. Cf. 32:3–5.
117. *DI* I, 16 (43:14–16).
118. Pseudo-Dionysius, *The Divine Names* V, 8 (*Dionysiaca* I, 355–356).
119. *IL* 33:4–5.
120. *IL* 32:7–8.
121. E.g., cf. *DI* II, 5 (119:11) with II, 1 (97:15–17). Cf. I, 6 (15:8–9); II, 1 (91:9–10); II, 6 (125:9–10). Also note the discussion about number in *DI* I, 5. Passages such as *DI* I, 13 (36:5–6) and I, 16 (42:4–5) do, however, mislead.
122. R. Klibansky, ed., *Ap.*, p. 32n.: "The [foregoing] opinions are quite often found in Augustine's works, though the [exact] words nowhere are."
123. *Ap.* 31:21–23. Regarding the attack on Parmenides see *IL* 33:32–33.
124. See corollary 2 of thesis 6—especially *IL* 34:33–35:2.
125. Pseudo-Dionysius, *The Mystical Theology* V (*Dionysiaca* I, 600).
126. See corollary 3 of thesis 6—especially *IL* 35:19–20.
127. See corollary 2 of thesis 7—especially *IL* 36:14–15.
128. *IL* 38:7–8.
129. *IL* 38:14.
130. Pseudo-Dionysius, *The Divine Names* VII, 4 (*Dionysiaca* I, 411).
131. *Ibid.* (*Dionysiaca* I, 413–414).
132. Pseudo-Dionysius, *The Divine Names* VII, 3 (*Dionysiaca* I, 404).
133. Cf. Rom. 8:35.
134. II Cor. 6:9.

APPENDIX

DE IGNOTA LITTERATURA
by
John Wenck

19

VENERABILI ET RELIGIOSO VIRO
DOMINO IOHANNI DE GEILHUSEN
OLIM ABBATI IN MULBRUNN, FAUTORI SUO SINGULARI.

Praeamande pater, visa Docta Ignorantia mihi nuper
5 praesentata, trium libellorum partialium satis eleganti stilo con-
fecta, quae incipit "Admirabitur, et recte, maximum tuum et iam
probatissimum ingenium" et terminatur "eo aeternaliter fruituri,
qui est in saecula benedictus. Amen.", provocor ego ipse Ignotam
conscribere Litteraturam, qua per oppositum ad has quas praefata
10 Docta Ignorantia tractat materias, meo iudicio insalutariter, de
Deo, de universo ac Ihesu Christo, ex ea ingressus pateat in
potentias Domini, ad memorandam eius iustitiam, quam ignorantes
inobedienter suam statuerunt, ait apostolus Romanorum X°. Et laborem
huius suscepti operis forsitan alleviabit aeternae vitae promissio facta
15 divinitus veritatis elucidatoribus, de supererogationis redditione
Lucae X°, cum eo quod scriptum est Ecclesiastici XXIV°: "Qui eluci-
dant me vitam aeternam habebunt."

Ad hanc quoque Ignotam Litteraturam evigilabunt animi legentium
ex innata cupidine salutis. Armis autem spiritalibus Doctae Ignorantiae
20 quaedam dicta impugnaturus veluti fidei nostrae dissona, piarum mentium
offensiva, necnon ab obsequio divino vaniter abductiva. In caput dicendorum
occurrit illud Psalmi XLV°, "Vacate et videte quoniam ego sum
Deus," pro legitima registratione totius nostrae mentalis negotiationis
Nam, dum prophetae intueor mentem, ablatis bellis malae volun-
25 tatis Deo nostro repugnantibus, insuper et insidiarum confractis
armis, pacificantis Christi nostri propugnatoris habenda notitia,
20 indicitur quia "vacate et videte quoniam ego sum Deus." Con-
sideravit namque quosdam vacantes sed ad otium nutriendum

---

19 6 quae incipit: *in margine T*   14 alleviabit: *partim obscurum est in T*   15 e-
lucidatoribus: *partim obscurum est in T*   16 scriptum: *partim obscurum est in T*
20 nostrae: nostra *M*   22 Psalmi XLV°: Psalmi XLI *M* Psalmus XLI *T*   25 repugnantibus: repungnantibus *T*   26 pacificantis: paficantis *M*

in vinea Domini, qui increpantur Matthaei XX°: "Quid hic statis
tota die otiosi?" Vident et plurimi, sed non ad salutem, finem
5 fidei nostrae, sed ad curiositatem et vanitatem; de quibus Romanorum I°:
"Evanuerunt in cogitationibus suis, et obscuratum est insipiens cor
eorum." A quibus nos Dominus Deus cupiens elongare, excludere,
et sequestrare, otium et visionem nostras in seipsum reflectens,
nobis imperat vacare ad quiete videndum—non quidem in nuda stando
10 visione scientiali nos inflante (a qua et daemones graeco vocabulo
nuncupantur, daemones enim interpretantur scientes) sed potius
visionis vacantia tendendo in id quod vere Deus est, omnis nostrae
motionis satians requietio. Pulchre ergo determinans vacare,
addidit expositive "et videte," attexens causaliter quid videndum:
15 "quoniam ego sum Deus," ubi "ego" singularizans omnem creaturam patenter a divinitate excludit, Deum ab omni distinguens
creatura, quia ipse Deus creator, non creatura. Rectificatum ergo
est ex themate totum nostrae mentis negotiandi exercitium Ignotae
Litteraturae pernecessarium respectu conflictus ineundi contra
20 Doctam Ignorantiam.

Gloriatur vir iste doctae ignorantiae, cardinalem alloquens,
se invenisse quod dudum variis doctrinarum viis concupiverit in
mari, in reditu de Graecia, ductu superni luminis. Et subspeci-
ficans illud suum inventum ait: ut incomprehensibilia incom-
25 prehensibiliter amplecterer in docta ignorantia per transcensum
veritatum incorruptibilium humanitus scibilium, quam se dicit
tribus libellis in eo qui veritas est absolvisse. Sed hortatur nos
discipulus quem diligebat Ihesus, canonica sua prima, capitulo IV°,
non credere omni spiritui sed probare spiritus an ex Deo sint,
30 annectens necessitatis causam: "quoniam multi pseudoprophetae
exierunt in mundum." De quibus apostolus II^a Corintheorum XI° sub-
specificantius loquens ait: "pseudoapostoli operarii subdoli trans-
figurantes se in apostolos Christi"; de quorum numero forsan
extat vir iste doctae ignorantiae, callide sub specie religionis decipiens
21 eos qui nondum exercitatos habent sensus. Nam ex quo spiritu
haec docta procedat ignorantia, dudum iam Waldensica, Eckhardica,
atque Wiclefica praemonstraverunt doctrinationes.

Iubemur a Salvatore, Marci primo, evangelio credere, quoniam

20 4 finem: *om. T*   11 interpretantur: interpretatur *M*   12 Deus: *bis T* (Deus[1] *del. T*)   16 distinguens: dxstingwens *M* distigwens *T*   19 ineundi: eundi *T*   26 quam: *partim destructum T*

De Ignota Litteratura

5 est Dei sermo indissolubilis, Iohannis X°: "Non potest solvi scriptura."
Cuius assertio ab apostolo praeponitur angelico evangelio, ad Galathas I°:
"Licet nos aut angelus de caelo evangelizet vobis praeterquam quod
evangelizavimus vobis, anathema sit." Dicit autem evangelium,
Iª Corintheorum XIII°, nos intelligere per speculum in aenigmate.
10 Quomodo ergo in hac vita incomprehensibilia incomprehensibiliter
apprehenderemus? Repugnat namque in hac vita, ubi secundum
Boetium "omne quod recipitur recipitur secundum modum reci-
pientis," aliter hominem comprehendere quam comprehensibiliter
et in imagine, cum, ex III° De Anima, hoc sit phantasma ad intel-
15 lectum quod est color ad visum. Constat autem sine lumine coloris
actuante obiectaliter visum nihil posse videre; ergo nec sine
phantasmate contingit nos intelligere. Quapropter scriptura sancta
in symbolis nobis tradidit divinitus inspirata ac revelata pariformiter
ad consuetudinem naturalis nostrae conceptionis.
20   Verum hic scriba doctae ignorantiae, ut omnem evadat argumen-
torum impugnationem, hanc dat cautelam: ut in huiusmodi
profundis incomprehensibilibus incomprehensibiliter amplectendis
omnis nostri humani ingenii conatus se ad illam elevet simplicitatem ubi contradictoria coincidunt, in quo dicit laborare primi
25 sui libelli conceptum. Quam simplicitatem dicit Deum, non videns
illud quod in themate praemissum est, "quoniam ego sum Deus,"
cum quo nihil creaturae coincidit aut ex rei natura commiscetur.
Et si praefatus magister doctae ignorantiae omnem sic praevenire vult
oppositionem, tunc nulla erit ibidem contradictio. Et quis eum
30 redarguet?, cum tunc nulla possit fundari consequentia, deficiente
repugnantia oppositi consequentis ad antecedens. Ubi tunc erunt
consequentiae prophetarum Salvatoris, evangelistarum, ac aposto-
lorum, quibus dinoscitur fides non modicum roborata contra per-
fidos? Affert etiam de medio talismodi eius assertio semen omnis
22 doctrinae, videlicet illud: Idem esse et non esse impossibile, IV°
Metaphysicae. Verum hic homo parum curat de dictis Aristotilicis,
quia fatetur se ex eodem fundamento semper progredi et rara
multis super communem viam philosophorum elicuisse. Unde Ihesus
5 Dominus maior factus sit sibi in intellectu et affectu per fidei
incrementum.

21 7 evangelizet: *habet* v ewangelii et *MT*   8 evangelizavimus: *habet* v evangelizaverimus *M* ewangelizaverimus *T*   11 Repugnat: Repungnat *T*   16 nec: *supra lin. T*   nec sine: sine nec sine *M*   21 ut: michi *post* ut *scribit et del. T*   29 oppositionem: opinionem *T*   33 roborata: reborata *M*

22 3 fatetur: fature *M*   fundamento: fudamento *M* (*litteram* m *non proprie format M*)

Iohannes Wenck

Dicit autem illud suum fore fundamentum: videlicet, in simplicissima et abstractissima intelligentia unum esse omnia; ex quo ibi omnia omne quod differentialitatis est oportet evomere.
10 Elicita autem per eum ex hoc fundamento in conclusiones et correlaria ob ampliorem memoriae capacitatem collegi; de quibus in subsequentibus per ordinem tractabo, antea tamen in primis declarando quare huic scripto titulum hunc, scilicet Ignota Litteratura, praefixerim.
15 Quod si nativum nostrum addiscendi animadvertimus modum: cum praefato scriba doctae ignorantiae, in praeambulari elucidatione, primo convenio in facie sensibili desiderii sciendi, hac videlicet: quemadmodum tristis sensatio in orificio stomachi praecedens naturam stimulat ad refici, ita admirari irritat sciendi desiderium
20 omnibus hominibus naturaliter inditum. Sic enim scriptum est I° Metaphysicae: "Omnes homines natura scire desiderant." Et iterum: "Propter admirari ceperunt antiqui philosophari." Et quia ad huiusmodi naturalem inclinationem sciendi ut executioni demandetur ne sit frustra sed ut in amato pondere propriae naturae quietem
25 attingat, oportet inquisitionis seu investigationis scientialis modum aperire—in quo iterum cum saepe fato scriba doctae ignorantiae concordo. Qui est: omnes investigantes in comparatione sive habitudine sive proportione praesuppositi sive propositi certi proportionaliter incertum iudicant, quia hoc est logicae officium,
30 quae II° Metaphysicae dicitur sciendi modus dirigere et docere mentem devenire in suo discursu de noto ad ignoti notitiam attingendam. Sic ergo omnis inquisitio rationis comparativa est seu collativa, utens medio proportionis. Hinc singula inquirenda, venanda, vel investiganda veniunt iudicanda et cognoscenda ex proportionali
35 sive comparativa reductione incerti, ignoti, sive incogniti quod inquiritur, ad praesuppositum sive propositum certum, notum, manifestum, et cognitum, ut innotescat et manifestetur. Unde ratio-
23 nalis discursionis inchoatio sive inceptio aut initium est a noto, terminatio autem ac finis est ad ignotum manifestandum. Quapropter ipse in titulo sui libelli utrumque inquisitionis sive discursionis terminum complectitur, quia "docta," ecce notum, "igno-
5 rantia," ecce ignotum. Similiter ego in titulo huius libelli, qui est

22 11 correlaria: *abbreviatum M (ut semper)* ampliorem: *habet v* amphorem *M* anphorem *T*   15 animadvertimus: animaadvertimus *M*   36 notum: sive *add. T*
37 innotescat: innotestat *T*

De Ignota Litteratura

"ignota," ecce terminum ad quem, "litteratura," ecce terminum a quo, eiusdem mentalis investigationis.

Nec hic titulus per me noviter est adinventus, sed dudum a sanctis prophetis divinitus inspiratis enuntiatus, cum apud
10 Isaiam, capitulo XXIX°, "Liber signatus dabitur nescienti litteras," et David, Psalmo LXX°, se fateatur "non cognovisse litteraturam" et tamen "intraturum in potentias Domini, iustitiae solius Dei memoraturum." Haec enim ignota litteratura, teste Isaia refellens doctrinas hominum, perire facit sapientiam a sapientibus et abscondet intellectum
15 a prudentibus quorum in tenebris sunt opera, ubi pulchre dixit Isaias: "quorum in tenebris sunt opera"; quia quod in artibus male operatur non est artis culpa, quae lux est et vitium nescit, sed hominis male agentis, cuius conversatio non in lumine sed in tenebris.

20 Ex praemissis ergo praefatus scriba doctae ignorantiae emulationem sive zelum sciendi habere satis ostenditur; sed quod non secundum scientiam subsequentia declarabunt.

Dicit namque scire esse ignorare, cum habitus et privatio distinguantur; immo in termino ad quem, in quo quies, privatio
25 abiecta est, quae habitui acquisitio repugnabat.

Dicit ulterius: non conspicimus ipsam simplicissimam entitatem, quae est essentia omnium, nisi in doctissima ignorantia. Ex quo docta notitia, ex superius fundatis, proportionem includit, et per consequens numerum et finitatem, quae in simplicissima enti-
30 tate, eo quod infinita omnem aufugiens et superfugiens proportionem, locum non habet. Cum enim simplicissima entitas non admittat excedens et excessum, tunc est super omne quod per nos concipi potest. Et sic cum ex finitis transsumptio fiat ad infinitissimum et ab omni figura absolutissimum, tunc illud nostra
35 ignorantia incomprehensibiliter edocebit, linquens sensibilia quae
24 transcendit, in inapprehensibilem veritatem incomprehensibiliter expedite ascendens.

Cui respondeo per illud Sapientiae XIII°: "A magnitudine speciei creaturae cognoscibiliter poterit creator videri." Delectatus decore
5 creaturarum, David ait se psallere "quia delectasti me, Domine, in factura tua," Psalmo XCI°, ubi non excludit facturam sive creaturam neque repudiat,

---

23 7 investigationis: *non proprie scribit* M   8 adinventus: inventus T   10 Isaiam: Ysaiam M   Ysayam T   11 Psalmo: Psalmus T   13 Isaia: Ysaya MT   16 Isaias: Ysaias M   Ysayas T   21 sive: seu T   24 distinguantur: distigwantur MT   28 quo: quo (*et non* quomodo) *habet, ut videtur,* T   30 infinita omnem: omnem infineitatem T   32 super: nos *post* super *scribit et del.* M

qui iubet Dominum laudare in sanctis eius, Psalmo ultimo. Sic ergo scriba
doctae ignorantiae, intrans caliginem tenebrarum, linquens omnem speciem
et decorem creaturarum, evanescit in cogitationibus. Et non valens
10 Deum intueri sicuti est, quia adhuc viator, ipsum nequaquam
glorificat. Sed in tenebris suis eans, culmen divinae laudis ad
quod omnis psalmodia perducitur derelinquit et postponit. Quod
fore nefandissimum et incredulum quis fidelium ignorat? Ad
hunc tamen errorem eum paucitas instructionis logicae induxit,
15 qua putavit in sua ignorantia adaequatam et praecisam ad Deum proportionem tamquam medium Deum venandi et noscendi se recepisse.
  Venio nunc specialius ad eius dicta per conclusiones et
correlaria.
  Prima conclusio: Omnia cum Deo coincidunt. Patet, quia
20 est maximum absolutum, non admittens excedens et excessum.
Ergo nihil sibi oppositum; et per consequens, ob defectum dis-
cretionis, ut ait Hermes Tresmagistus, ipse est universitas rerum.
Et per consequens etiam nullum nomen ei proprie potest convenire,
ob defectum discretivae impositionis, cum impositio nominis sit a
25 determinata qualitate eius cui nomen imponitur.
  Huic conclusioni alludit magister Eghardus in libro suo vulgari quem
edidit pro regina Ungariae, sorore ducum Austriae, quod incipit "Benedictus
Deus et pater Domini nostri Ihesu Christi," dicens: "Homo deberet
esse multum diligens ut spoliaret et denudaret se ipsum a propria
30 imagine et cuiuscumque creaturae et ignoraret patrem nisi solum
25 Deum; tunc nihil est quod possit eum contristare vel conturbare,
nec Deus, nec creatura, nec aliquod creatum, nec aliquod increatum:
totum suum esse, vivere, et nosse, scire, amare est ex Deo, in Deo,
et Deus." Et idem in sermonibus suis: "In anima est quoddam
5 castellum quod interdum vocavi custodiam animae quandoque
scintillam, et valde simplex sicut Deus est unus et simplex. Ita
simplex est et super omnem modum quod deus non potest
intueri secundum modum et proprietates personales. Et si intueretur
ipsum, hoc constaret: eum [super] omnia sua nomina divina et suas pro
10 prietates personales, eo quod ipse est sine modo et
proprietate. Sed secundum quod ipse Deus est unus et simplex

---

24 11 tenebris suis: tenebras suas *M*   14 logicae: logicem *M*   22 Tresmagistus: Tremagistus *MT*   23 proprie potest: potest proprie *T*
25 9 super: *supplevi*   10 ipse: *habet v*   ipsum *MT*   11 quod: *bis M*

De Ignota Litteratura

et sine modo et proprietate, secundum quod nec est Pater, nec Filius, nec Spiritus Sanctus, sic potest ipse intrare in illud unum quod voco castellum."

15 Aspice quanta mala in huiusmodi docta ignorantia simplicissima atque abstractissima intelligentia scaturiunt et ebulliunt! Unde Iohannes, episcopus Argentinensis, anno Domini 1317, sabbato ante festum Assumptionis Beatae Mariae Virginis, dedit processum contra Beghardos et sorores in sua civitate, dicentes Deum esse
20 formaliter omne quod est et se esse Deum per naturam sine distinctione.

Nec valet probatio conclusionis adductae, quia illa cum conclusione tolleret penitus benedictam Trinitatem, ex quo in illo maximo absoluto, quod Deus est, secundum ipsum scribam doctae
25 ignorantiae, nulla est discretio nec relationis oppositio. Et sic personae in divinis proprietatibus non differrent; et per consequens in hac docta ignorantia nedum divinarum personarum esset confusio sed etiam universitatis rerum cum Deo esset essentialis unio.

Quod nedum constat esse contra fidem orthodoxam, verum etiam
30 contra semetipsum, qui postea in suo libro benedictam Trinitatem nititur similitudinibus astruere, quas tamen sua docta ignorantia praescidit et reliquit. Et si sic est universorum praecisio a Deo ut ipse asserit in aspectu simplicissimae entitatis essentiae omnium doctissimae ignorantiae, quomodo ipsemet in hac prima conclusione connectit Deo omnia
35 coincidenter?

26 Correlarium primum huius primae conclusionis: Maximitate absoluta omnia sunt id quod sunt, eo quod illa est entitas absoluta sine qua nihil esse nequit. Huic sic alludit Eghardus in scripto suo super Genesim et Exodum: "Esse est Deus, quia si esset
5 aliud ab ipso Deo, Deus non esset, aut si esset, alio utique esset." Et subdit: "Principium in quo creavit Deus caelum et terram est primum nunc simplex aeternitatis, ipsum inquam idem nunc penitus in quo Deus est ab aeterno, in quo etiam est, fuit, et erit aeternaliter personarum emanatio. Unde cum quaereretur a me aliquando
10 quare Deus mundum non creasset prius, respondi: quia non potuit, eo quod non esset nec fuerat prius antequam esset mundus; quomodo poterat creare prius, cum in eodem nunc mox mundum creavit in quo fuit Deus?"

25 16 ebulliunt: ebuliunt *T*   17 Unde: Und *M*   1317: 1417 *T*   18 Assumptionis: Assumpcionis *ex* Annunciacionis *corr. T*   33 simplicissimae: simplicissime *ex* simplicitate *corr. T*

26 2 absoluta: absoluta *scribit improprie, del., et rescribit, T*   3 Eghardus: Eckhardus *T*   4 et: *supra lin. T*   8 est[2]: *om. T*   9 personarum: aliquando *ante* personarum *scribit et del. T*

Iohannes Wenck

Attendant hi errantes illud Sapientiae XI°: "Omnia in mensura et
numero et pondere disposuisti. Multum enim valere tibi soli
supererat semper; et virtuti brachii tui quis resistet? Quoniam
tamquam momentum staterae, sic ante te est orbis terrarum, et
tamquam gutta roris antelucani" (antelucanus una dictio, id est, ante
lucem existens, ut lucanus est splendor matutinus) "quae descendit
in terram." Auferret ergo hoc correlarium subsistentias rerum
in proprio genere, quae virtute Dei ne in nihilum fluant manutenentur, dicente apostolo Hebraeorum I°: "omnia portans verbo
virtutis suae." Et si manutenentur a Deo, tunc utique non sunt
Deus, maximitas scilicet absoluta, sed sunt aliquid et non nihil,
et distincta a Deo eorum creatore.

Correlarium secundum huius primae conclusionis eiusdem doctae
ignorantiae: Haec maximitas absoluta omnia habet in se, et ipsa est
in omnibus, quia sua universitate omnia complectitur, quemadmodum natura, quae est contracta, est quasi explicatio omnium quae
per motum fiunt.

Universalizantes ob simplicitatem universalis naturae quam
ponunt in re representant omnia essentialiter deificari in huiusmodi praecisa abstractione. Quod tamen et divinae repugnat sim-
plicitati, et compositionem realem Deo ex creaturis inducit, quod
horrendum est dicere, cum illa aeterna et infinita perfectio quae
Deus est non habet quo crescat aut decrescat. Nam sicut ema-
nando non deficit, sic nec in recursu seu reductione creaturarum
ad ipsum essentialiter superabundat.

Secunda conclusio eiusdem doctrinae ignorantiae: Praecisa veritas
est incomprehensibilis, cum careat proportione ad praesuppositum
certum deveniendi ad incertum, ex quo est infinita. Infinitum autem,
secundum quod infinitum, est ignotum.

Mirandum valde, cum prius dixit simplicissimam entitatem,
quae est essentia omnium, conspici in doctissima ignorantia, qua
incomprehensibilia incomprehensibiliter amplectuntur. Cum eadem
simplicissima entitas videatur praecisa veritas, quomodo incomprehensibilis et incomprehensibiliter amplexibilis? Fundamentum autem

---

26 16 supererat: *habet v* superat *MT*   17 staterae: statera *T*   18 antelucani: ante lucem *T*   19 ut: *ex* unde *supra lin. corr. T*   quae: qui *T*   22 portans: potestas *MT*   23 manutenentur: mautenentur *M*   31 naturae: nature *scribit non plene legibiliter, del., et rescribit, T*   32 representant: representat *M*   33 repugnat: repungnat *T*

27 2 sic: *habet v* sicut *MT*   3 essentialiter: respondetur *M*   12 incomprehensibiliter: inapprehensibiliter *T*

De Ignota Litteratura

huius conclusionis annullaret scientiam divinorum. Intelligatur ergo
hic in scientiis duplex modus determinandi: compositivus scilicet,
descendendo a primis in ultima per compositionem secundi cum
primo et sic deinceps; et resolutorius, dividendo causata in primas
causas et composita in simplicia. Modo suprema causa et simplicissima Deus. Ex hoc quod creaturae sunt eius effectus et effectus
gerit similitudinem suae causae, tunc ut docetur I° Sententiarum:
Deus in vestigio et in imagine est cognoscibilis sub notione similitudinis creaturarum innotescens, quia per scripturam sub similitudinibus creaturarum nobis descriptus idonee ad nostram comprehensionem eo modo quo hic in via comprehendi potest. Unde
et ipsa praecisa veritas, in eo quod praecisa, habitudinem importat
et proportionem ad alias veritates non praecisas, sicut et maximitas
absoluta ad maximitates habitudinibus concretas. Nec oportet in
medio scientiali habere adaequatam proportionem, quia illa esset
identitas potius quam similitudo.

Correlarium primum huius conclusionis secundae: Non possunt
duo aut plura adeo similia et aequalia reperiri quin adhuc in infinitum similiora esse possint. Patet ex aequalitate graduali qua
unum aequalius est uni quam alteri secundum convenientiam et
differentiam genericam, specificam, localem, influentialem, et temporalem cum similibus. Exemplum de polygonio ad circulum.

Istud correlarium destruit statum in causis et distinctionem
entium in proprio genere. Unde cum ex Praedicamentis aequalitas
fundetur in quantitate et similitudo in qualitate, et reperiatur
quantitas molis sive magnitudinis et quantitas virtutis, et potentiae
finitae sint I° Caeli, et similiter quodlibet praedicamentorum in
generalissimo et suo specialissimo, ut docet Porphirius, quomodo
tunc ponere potest aliquid in infinitum similius aut aequalius, cum
etiam distincta sint ad maximum et minimum? I° Physicorum.
Ex comparatione tamen cuiuslibet ad quodlibet, magnum haberetur
fundamentum intentionalis memoriae, de qua alibi discussio.

Correlarium secundum eiusdem secundae conclusionis: Finitus
intellectus rerum veritatem per similitudinem non potest praecise

---

27 13 huius: huiusmodi *T*   14 duplex: dux *M*
28 2 polygonio: *habet* v   pologonia *MT*   3 distinctionem: determinationem *M*
7 sint: sicut *T*   9 cum: *aut* cum *aut* tum *habet M*   10 distincta: determinata *M*
Physicorum: Phylosophorum *T*   11 quodlibet: quotlibet *T*   haberetur: haberetur
habet *T* (*abbreviatio pro* ur *non deleta est in T*)

Iohannes Wenck

15 attingere, cum semper sit inter mensuram et mensuratum,
quantumcumque aequalia, manens differentia.
Clarum est apud Aristotelem ea quae scimus minima esse
eorum quae ignoramus, et intellectum nostrum videre in imagine
et similitudine, nec aequalitatem et similitudem identitatem
20 posse fieri; nihilominus tamen manens differentia in comparatis
ad invicem non tollit scientiam. Quod ergo veritatem vult per
similitudinem non posse praecise sive indivisibiliter intellectum attingere. Quid est illud dicere [aliud] quam quod non nude sed umbratice
eandem intelligit, quod est consonum et philosophiae et theologiae, et
25 infirmitatem nostrae cognitionis fateri?

Conclusio tertia eiusdem doctrinae ignorantiae: Quidditas
rerum, quae est entium veritas, in sua puritate est inattingibilis,
quia semper intellectio in infinitum purificari et praescindi potest.

Iam ante dictum est quod veritas rerum a nostro intellectu
30 in imagine et similitudine concipitur; intellectus enim possibilis,
ex III° De Anima, locus est specierum intellectibilium. Et prius dictum est superiore quod videre rem in sua puritate sicuti est, non
est viae sed patriae. Sed homo ille doctae ignorantiae vult in eadem
docta ignorantia, sequestrata omni similitudine, rem in sua puri-
35 tate intelligere. Intelligibilis tamen adhuc est quidditas sive veritas
29 rerum, quia ex quo quod quid est, est obiectum intellectus, ex
III° De Anima, tunc in illud est naturaliter latio intellectus. Et si
esset inattingibile, motus ille intellectualis esset sine termino ad
quem, et per consequens non [finis] motus, et per consequens infinitus
5 et frustra, quod esset destruere propriam operationem intellectus.
Nec assumpta conclusionis probatio valet, cum non in infinitum
intellectio praescindi poterit ex particula diffinitionis scientiae mate-
rialis, primo Posteriorum, hac videlicet, quoniam illius est causa.

Correlarium primum huius conclusionis tertiae: In maximo
10 simpliciter nedum minimum coincidit sed et contradictoria quae-
vis combinantur, connectuntur, et uniuntur concorditer. Patet.
Cum sit omne illud quod esse potest, id est possibilia omnia in

---

28 19 nec: *habet v* ut *MT*   23 Quid: *habet v* Quod *MT*   aliud: *supplevi*
non: *supra lin. T*   28 praescindi: prescindi *habet v* prescidi *MT*   30 enim:
supra lin. M   31-32 dictum est: dictum est *v* d̄t est *M*   dicunt esse *T* (dicunt *ex*
d̄t *corr. T*)   32 superiore: sup^e *MT*   videre: est *post* videre *scribit et del. T*

29 4 consequens[1]: consequenciam (?) *T*   finis: *supplevi*   7 praescindi: prescindi *habet v*   prescidi *MT*   9 huius: prime *post* huius *scribit et del. T*

De Ignota Litteratura

actu, tunc est penitus in actu quidquid est; nec sit ibi excedens
aut excessum nec oppositio.

15   O quantum spargitur hic venenum erroris et perfidiae, correlario isto destruente omnem processum scientificum ac omnem consequentiam, pariter et tollente omnem oppositionem, pariter et legem contradictionis, et per consequens totam doctrinam Aristotelis, destructo semine omnis doctrinae, de quo supra. Nec valet
20   quod pro probatione assumitur, quod Deus sit omne quod est, quia tunc creatione eius nec caelum nec terra nec aliae creaturae processissent de nihilo in esse, cuius oppositum legislator Moyses in Genesi doctrinat.

   Correlarium secundum eiusdem conclusionis tertiae: Omne quod
25   concipitur esse non magis est quam non est. Patet, quia maximum absolutum ita est hoc quod est omnia, quod est et nullum.

   Quod siquidem correlarium destruit Deum esse; ex quo enim Deus concipitur, tunc non magis est quam non est. Et iterum in probatione astruit Deum esse creaturam. Non ergo magister hic
30   doctae ignorantiae vacat et videt, iuxta iussum superius assumpti thematis quod dicit Deus: "quoniam ego sum Deus." Immo plus desipit olim Beghardis Argentinensibus per eorum episcopum damnatis, qui dicebant se esse Deum per naturam sine distinctione, et quod in eis essent omnes perfectiones divinae, et essent
35   aeterni et in aeternitate. Qui et dicebant se omnia creasse et plus
30   quam Deus, et nullo indigere, nec Deo nec deitate, dicentes: "Si vis adorare Deum, adora me."

   Quarta conclusio eiusdem doctae ignorantiae: Quod spiritualia per se a nobis inattingibilia symbolice investigentur, hanc habet
5   radicem: quoniam omnia ad se invicem quandam, nobis tamen occultam et incomprehensibilem, habent proportionem, ut ex omnibus unum exurgat universum et omnia in uno maximo sint unum, cum similitudo exemplaris sit hoc ipsum quod exemplar in unitate naturae.
10   O quanta infirmitas intellectus, omnia asserere unum esse, et omnia essentialiter deificari, nec imaginem posse distinguere a suo exemplari! Cum enim imago ad similitudinem accedit sui exemplaris, non ad identitatem, tunc non est hoc ipsum quod est exemplar in unitate naturae. Sic dicebant Lolhardi Argen-
15   tinenses damnati, quod homo possit sic uniri Deo quod ipsius

29 20 assumitur: sumitur *ante* assumitur *scribit et del.* M   32 Beghardis: *ex* Beghardiis *corr.* T
30 2 me: *bis* M (me² *del.* M)   5 tamen: *non proprie abbreviat* M   7 universum: universis T   11 distinguere: destingwere M   distigwere T

sit idem posse et velle et operari quodcumque quod est ipsius
Dei. Immo Eghardus in sermonibus suis ait: "Pater generat
filium suum in me," et "Ego sum ibi ille idem filius, non alius."
Quae omnia tam abominanda sunt, quod ea refugit fidelis intel-
20 lectus tractare nisi in defensionem fidei professae.
  Correlarium primum conclusionis quartae: Cum ipsum simpliciter maximum symbolice investigare proponimus, simplicem
similitudinem transilire necesse est. Patet, cum ipsum maximum nihil horum esse possit quae per nos sciuntur aut conci-
25 piuntur, quia indifferentiatum et praecisum.
  Illud correlarium sine similitudine vult Deum intelligere et tamen ex probatione non intelligere Deum, quod implicat
[contradictionem]. Unde et futuro statui facialis Dei visio, quam
hic transiliendo similitudinem intelligere videtur, reservata est.
30 I^a Iohannis III°: Tunc "videbimus eum sicuti est."
  Correlarium secundum eiusdem conclusionis quartae: Nostra
ignorantia incomprehensibiliter docebit quomodo de altissimo
rectius et verius sit nobis in aenigmate laborantibus sentiendum.
Patet, quia illa est ab omni figura absolutissima pariter et tran-
35 scendens rationes finitarum et comparatarum rerum.
31 Rogo quomodo ignorantia docet, cum docere sit actus doctrinae positivus? Nec valet probatio, quia absolvi ab omni forma
non convenit ignorantiae, quae numquam habuit formam qua nuda-
retur. Hoc ergo correlarium destructivum est omnis scientiae, ex-
5 tollendo nostram ignorantiam supra omnem doctrinam. Neque
etiam valet probatio quam facit capitulo II° primi libri, quod
ignorare sit scire, quia Socrati visum sit se nihil scire nisi quod
ignoraret, seu etiam quia omnis inquisitio utitur proportione noti
ad ignoti notitiam; quoniam nec doctor gentium iudicans se
10 nihil scire inter Corintheos nisi Ihesum Christum et hunc cruci-
fixum, alias scientias abnegavit, quibus abundabat, sed eisdem
ignotam praetulit litteraturam libri signati, qui est Christus Ihesus.
Socrates namque dicendo scire se nihil scire, astruxit scire, ab-
negans completum scire, sive profitens diminutum scire, per hoc
15 insinuans habere se desiderium sciendi quae nondum scivit sed
adhuc ignoravit. "Qui enim apponit scientiam, apponit et dolorem,"

30 16 et²: *om. T*   26 similitudine: quem *add. MT, sed*
dictionem: *add. v; cf. 33:4*   35 et: non *add. T*

De Ignota Litteratura

Ecclesiastae I° (sive ut habet communis translatio, "Qui addit scientiam, addit et dolorem"), quoniam scientia acquisita incendium praebet amplius sciendi, iuxta illud Ecclesiastici XXIV°: "Qui edunt
20 me adhuc esurient." Quomodo ergo doctrina expellens ignorantiam ab eadem exoriretur? cum privatio machinativa sit maleficii. Primo Physicorum. Ex quibus liquet quantam venenositatem scientiae et morum induxerit abstractissima illa intelligentia, nuncupata docta ignorantia, vulgariter "abgescheiden leben," in qua
25 sensuum est evanescentia, et postposita Dei glorificatio qua exaltatur Deus in gentibus et in terra, iuxta assumptum thema: "Vacate et videte quoniam ego sum Deus." Et sequitur: "Exaltabor in gentibus, et exaltabor in terra."

Quinta conclusio eiusdem doctae ignorantiae: Quidquid pos-
30 sibile est, hoc est actu ipsum maximum maxime, non ut ex possibili est, sed ut maxime est. Patet ex proportione, quia infinita linea non est triangulus ut ex finita educitur, sed actu est triangulus infinitus, qui idem est cum linea; ex quo possibilitas absoluta in maximo non est aliud quam ipsum maximum actu. Et dicit
32 ulterius quod omnis theologia per nos apprehensibilis ex hoc tanto principio elicitur.

Subvertit haec conclusio omnem theologizandi modum nobis per totam bibliam traditum, dicens ex hoc principio, scilicet quid-
5 quid possibile est esse actu ipsum maximum maxime, ex quo esse est maximum, elici omnem theologiam per nos apprehensibilem. Pro cuius principii probatione plura falsa asseruit, quia nulla linea est infinita, nec triangulus est linea, nec possibilitas est actus. Non ergo mirum si falsa ex falsis infert, cum, I° Physicorum,
10 uno inconvenienti dato, plura sequuntur. Unde, ex suis huiusmodi dictis, sequeretur quod nedum creatura quae est, sed quae possibilis est, esset Deus, contra thema assumptum: "Vacate et videte quoniam ego sum Deus."

Quid ergo hic scriba doctae ignorantiae aliud facit, nisi illis mediis
15 abducere homines a Dei cultu et sincera congrua devotione, quibus se ipsum dicit devocatum et inflammatum et in fide per amplius incensum, volens dare huiusmodi modum praefatum theologizandi, a vero modo theologizandi

---

31 17 Ecclesiastae: Ecclesiastici *MT*   18 dolorem: *ex* delorem *(?) corr. T*
22 Physicorum: et cetera *add. T*   24 abgescheiden: abgeschaiden *M*   34 aliud: aliud *conieci* ad *MT*
32 3 modum: principium *T*   11 sequeretur: sequereretur *M*   12 esset: esse *T*

Iohannes Wenck

valde hominem alienans. Quod si divinitus traditus modus theologizandi scripturae sanctae de medio auferetur, nonne cessaret testi-
20 monium Salvatoris de seipso datum, Iohannis V°: "Scrutamini scripturas in quibus putatis vitam aeternam habere; et illae sunt quae
testimonium perhibent de me"? Nonne Iª Petri II° exhor-
tamur concupiscere lac scripturae in crescentiam nostrae salutis?
Quod siquidem lac genitis in Christo tam necessarium est ad
25 salutem quod eius negligentia inducit perfidiam, dicente Salvatore,
Matthaei XXII°: "Erratis, nescientes scripturas neque virtutem Dei";
quia postposita scriptura sancta et Christi potenti infirmitate non
animadversa, in apparentibus negotiatur homo phantasiis in quibus
error. Galatharum V°, ubi ab apostolo sectae, quae graece dicuntur haereses,
30 enumerantur inter opera carnis detestanda, cum per oppositum,
lectionis scripturae sanctae diligentia, nascatur sapientia phantasias
desipientes depellens et ab eisdem, et Christi infirmitate, quae Dei
virtus est et omnibus hominibus fortior, tota fulciatur ecclesia, et
surgit nova in Christo vita, quem scripsit Moyses in lege et pro-
35 phete, Iohannis I°.
33   Correlarium primum eiusdem quintae conclusionis: Hoc ipsum
maximum non istud quidem est, et aliud non est, sed est omnia
et nihil omnium. Patet, quia ipsum est esse omnium.
   Hoc correlarium contradictionem implicat, scilicet maximum
5 absolutum esse omnia et nihil omnium, cum quodlibet omnium
aliquid sit, ex quo nihil non componit aut constituit creaturam,
quae creatione procreata est, et per Verbum omnia facta sunt,
Iohannis I°, sine quo nihil.
   Correlarium secundum eiusdem: In docta ignorantia [elegantia] verborum
10 fatuitas reputatur, et sapientia ignorantia, ex quo habent adiunc-
tam proportionem et finitam.
   Ecce confusum hominem et in tenebris ambulantem, qui,
proportione qua ascendere deberet ad intelligentiam perversa,
graditur viam ad insipientiam et fatuitatis ignorantiam.
15   Correlarium tertium: Non reperitur alia praecisa mensura
cuiuscumque essentiae quam essentia maximi simpliciter. Patet,
quia omnes aliae praecisiores et absolutiores esse possunt.
   Aspice quorsum hunc scribam doctae ignorantiae ducat sua

32 21 quae: qui *M*   24 genitis: gemitis *T*   26 Erratis: Erratis *scribit non plene legibiliter, del., et rescribit, T*   31 phantasias: fantasiias *(?) M*   fantasias *ex* fantasiis *corr. T*

33 9 elegantia: *supplevi*   13 perversa: perversam *T*   17 praecisiores: preciosiores *T*   18 hunc: habent *M*

De Ignota Litteratura

abstractiva cognitio! Nam si Deus, quam ponit essentiam maximi
20 simpliciter, praecisa est mensura cuiuscumque essentiae, quomodo
tunc incomparabiliter omnem excedet essentiam, et quomodo stabit illud X° Metaphysicae?: Primum in unoquoque genere metrum est
et mensura sequentium illius generis; ergo in quolibet genere est
propria et praecisa mensura.
25   Conclusio sexta eiusdem doctae ignorantiae: Ut in divinis
clarius concipiatur idem esse trinitas et unitas, sive non aliud
distinctio quam indistinctio, oportet simplici conceptu, quantum
hoc possibile est, complecti contradictoria ipsa et antecedenter
praevenire, et unum in principio suo simplicissimo, ipso scilicet
30 maximo simpliciter. Patet, quia in illo non est aliud distinctio et
indistinctio, sed indistinctio est distinctio, et pluralitas unitas, sicut
ait Parmenides Deum esse cui esse quodlibet quod est est esse
omne id quod est.
   Hac conclusione scriba iste bene ostendit se ignorantem
35 doctum, quoniam sicut simulata sanctitas est duplex iniquitas,
34 quia fictio non existentiae, ita docta haec ignorantia, ficta existentia
scientiae sive doctrinae, non existens doctrina, habet falsam doctrinae
apparentiam et cum hoc doctrinae deficientiam. Et ita haec sua docta
ignorantia erit duplex ignorantia sive biformis nescientia, quam
5 sic pro posse nitor rationibus in contrarium saepire et circumtexere,
ne post suas concupiscentias deordinatas doctrinandi, mundum
circumveniat, animadvertens istud Ecclesiastici XXXVI°, "Ubi non est
saepes, diripietur possessio"; quoniam haec sua conclusio, si non
circumclauderetur sanis doctrinis, auferens distinctionem in divinis,
10 interimit trinitatem, quam tamen nititur ostendere identificam
unitati; cum ex distinctione pluralitas exoriatur, et in divinis omnia
sint idem, ubi non obviat relationis oppositio. Et valde claudicat
huius conclusionis probatio, quod Deus sit cui esse quodlibet quod
est est esse [omne id quod est]; cum etiam secundum auctorem Causarum,
15 prima causa sit in quolibet praeterquam quod alicui misceatur. Et for-

33 22 metrum: metros *MT*   31 pluralitas: *habet v* pluralis *MT*   34 ignorantem: *habet v* ignorante *MT*   35 sicut: sic *T*
34 4 nescientia: nescienciam *M*   6 post: *abbreviationem pro* post *scribit improprie, del., et rescribit, T*   mundum: mudum *M*   7 circumveniat: recumveniat *M*   14 omne id quod est: *supplevi*   auctorem: autorem *T*   15 quod: *non proprie abbreviat M*

tassis hunc doctum scribam ignorantem indigesta antiquorum librorum decepit perlectio multiformis.

Correlarium primum eiusdem conclusionis sextae: In huiusmodi maximo simpliciter anguli aut trianguli numerari non pos-
20 sunt per unum, duo, tria; cum quilibet sit in quolibet, ut ait Filius, "Ego in Patre et Pater in me"; et omnes unum maximum, per quod omnem anteimus oppositionem.

Scienti philosophiam, manifestum est esse alium modum essendi cum dicitur trigonum in tetragono, aut sensitivum in intellectivo,
25 quam cum dicitur Filius in Patre. Ergo, tenete consilium apostoli, Hebraeorum XIII°: "Doctrinis variis et peregrinis nolite abduci," et annectitur causa: "Optimum enim est gratia stabilire cor," scilicet ne evagetur post concupiscentias adulterinas variarum doctrinarum.

30 Correlarium secundum eiusdem: In unitate Trinitatis tanta est identitas quod etiam omnes relativas oppositiones antecedit. Patet, quia ibi aliud et diversum identitati non opponuntur. Cum enim maximum infinitae sit unitatis, tunc omnia quae ei conveniunt sunt ipsum absque diversitate et alietate. Unde neque
35 Pater est, neque Filius, neque Spiritus Sanctus; neque generans, neque genita, neque procedens, quia non nisi infinitas.

Loquitur expresse contra symbolum Athanasii, in quo sic dicitur: "In hac Trinitate nihil prius aut posterius"; insuper et
5 Trinitatem essentialiter interimit esse Deum ab aeterno.

Correlarium tertium eiusdem: Quia Deus est omnium complicatio, etiam contradictoriorum, hinc, ex quo nihil potest Dei Providentiam effugere, tunc omnia ad eam relata sunt necessaria. Patet, quia omnia in Deo sunt Deus, qui est necessitas absoluta; et ita
10 necesse est Deum providisse quae providit. Posita enim explicatione, ponitur complicatio; Deus autem in sua simplicitate complicat omnium rerum universitatem. Unde et hoc nomen tetragrammaton, id est IV^{or} litterarum, scilicet, ioth, he, vau, he, conveniens Deo secundum propriam essentiam, interpretatur unus
15 et omnia, sive omnia uniter, sicut nunc complicat tempus, et tempus praesentia ordinata; et quies est unitas motum complicans, et motus est explicatio quietis sive quies seriatim ordinata; et ita Patrem Filium gignere fuit omnia in Verbo creare.

34 18 sextae: sexte *abbreviat, del., et perscribit,* T   22 oppositionem: *non proprie abbreviat* M *(cf. 29:17; 34:12)*   23 essendi: in *add.* MT   27 causa: *bis* M   32 et: *ex* est *supra lin. corr.* T
35 9 qui: qui *(?)* habet M   12-13 tetragrammaton: thetragramaton MT   13 he²: habet v   phe MT   14 essentiam: *non proprie abbreviat* M *(cf. 33:19 et 21)*

De Ignota Litteratura

Correlarium illud est perniciosum, nam tollit contingen-
tiam futurorum, contra Philosophum, IX° Perihermeniarum; et omnia
deificat, omnia annihilat, et annihilationem ponit deificationem,
dicit idem generare Filium et creaturas creare.
Conclusio septima: Creatura semper fuit, quando esse potuit;
ipsa enim creatura est esse Dei. Quis namque intelligere potest
Deum esse essendi formam, nec tamen immisceri creaturae sed
una omnium complicatio? Deus enim omnia est complicans in
hoc quod omnia in eo, et omnia explicans in hoc quod ipse in
omnibus. Exemplificat sicut numerus explicatio unitatis, punctus
perfectio magnitudinum, identitas diversitatis complicatio, et
aequalitas inaequalitatis, et simplicitas divisionum.
    Haec conclusio destruit creaturam, de cuius conditione est
non semper fuisse; et cum ipse Deus semper est, quomodo creatura est
ipsum esse Dei? Licet enim primum bonum exemplariter appetatur
in quolibet bono, non tamen illud primum bonum habet quo
crescat ex creaturis, dicente David ad Dominum: "Bonorum
meorum non eges." Sicut enim Ecclesiastes I°, "Omnia flumina intrant
in mare, et mare non redundat," sic nihil ex creaturis accrescit
divinae perfectioni.
    Correlarium eiusdem conclusionis: Pluralitas rerum exoritur
eo quod Deus est in nihilo. Patet, quia tolle Deum a creatura
et nihil remanet, sicut una facies in diversis speculis si tollatur,
nihil de imaginibus remanet.
    Istud correlarium destituit Deum a suo esse, cum esse in
nihilo nihil sit.
    Correlarium secundum: Quidditas solis absoluta non est
aliud a quidditate lunae. Patet, quoniam est ipse Deus qui est
entitas et quidditas absoluta omnium.
    Correlarium hoc nefandissimum est, quia et rerum quidditates
confundit et quidditatem omnium Deum dicit.
    Correlarium tertium: Licet universum non sit nec sol nec
luna, est tamen in sole sol et in luna luna. Patet, quia uni-

---

35 20 IX°: *ad* IX° *correxi* primo *MT*   Perihermeniarum: Physicorum *T*
26 una: *non clare scriptum M*   omnium: *ex* omnia *(?) corr. M*   31 creaturam: creatura *M*
36 2 Ecclesiastes: Ecc^ces *T*   3 in: *om. T*   9 suo: sua *M*

113

versum dicit unitatem plurium; ergo in pluribus est illa.
Correlarium illud omni dissonat philosophiae.
20 Conclusio octava: Quodlibet in universo est ipsum universum, quamvis universum in quolibet sit diverse et quodlibet in universo diverse. Patet, quia universum est in quolibet id quod est ipsum contracte. In qualibet enim creatura universum est ipsa creatura, sicut Socrates humanitas in Socrate.
25 Haec conclusio et contradicit tertio correlario conclusionis septimae per expressum, et implicat [contradictionem], cum pars integrativa non sit totum. Sicut autem exemplificat quod linea maxima contracta est contracte omnes figurae, nescit quid loquitur, quia suae abstractissimae intelligentiae adducit mathematicalia imaginibus concreta.
30 Correlarium primum eiusdem conclusionis octavae: Anima mundi est explicatio mentis divinae. Patet, quoniam omnia quae in Deo sunt unum exemplar, in anima mundi sunt plura et distincta; ita quod Deus est ut punctus centralis, anima autem mundi ut circulus.
37 Ecce quod animam essentialiter dissimplificat, de qua philosophi multum diversificantur.
Correlarium secundum: Absolutus motus est quies et Deus, quia ille complicat omnes motus, quos quies explicat ut circulus
5 centrum.
Hoc correlarium destruit primum motorem, contra Philosophum, VIII° Physicorum.
Conclusio nona: Deus est centrum mundi, terrae, omnium sphaerarum, atque omnium quae in mundo sunt, simul et circum-
10 ferentia infinita. Patet, cum ipse solus sit infinita aequalitas.
Subdit quod terra est nobilis stella maior luna.
Conclusio haec contradicit scientiae de caelo, nec adiectum prius umquam est auditum.
Correlarium primum: Deus est claritas absoluta cuius ignei-
15 tatem omnia quae sunt nituntur iuxta posse participare, in omnibus astris materialiter contracta et immaterialiter contracta in vita viventium vita intellectiva. Patet, cum Deus sit lux in quo non sunt tenebrae.
Hoc correlarium divinae derogat maiestati, et in probatione

36 20 Quodlibet: Quotlibet *T*   26 contradictionem: *add. v; cf. 33:4*   29 mathematicalia: mathematisalia *M*

De Ignota Litteratura

20 eius videtur clare quod scriba doctae ignorantiae similitudinem
accipit pro re.
Correlarium secundum: Maximum absolute est omnia possibilia actu absolute, et in hoc est infinitissimum absolute; et maximum ad genus et speciem contractum pariformiter est actu possibilis
25 perfectio secundum datam contractionem. Exemplum est de
maxima linea, cum qua punctum coincidit; et ita maximum
contractum pariter et absolutum est Deus, et creaturas omnium
perfectionum complicans.
Correlarium hoc potentiam et actum identificat, contra
30 Philosophum, IX° Metaphysicae.
Correlarium tertium: Maximum contractum quod in se
complicat omnem perfectionem contractionis illius naturae nihil
adicit ipsi absolutae maximitati. Patet, quia maximitas absoluta
non est alia aut diversa, cum sit omnia.
38   Illud correlarium creaturam adaequat creatori.
Correlarium quartum: Ihesus complectitur omnes creaturas.
Patet, cum sit maximus homo in quo omnia, quia Deus, vivum
sicut mortuum complicans, quemadmodum lux corporalis hypostasis
5 est omnium colorum.
Possem hic uti verbis beati Iohannis Apocalypsis III° [adversus] scribam
hunc doctae ignorantiae: "Miser es et miserabilis et pauper et caecus
et nudus. Suadeo tibi emere aurum ignitum probatum ut non
appareat confusio nuditatis tuae. Collirio inunge oculos tuos ut
10 videas." Caret enim collirio, humanitatem scilicet Christi non
intelligens, quae est collirium oculorum nostrorum videndi Dei
gloriam, ut ait malleus haereticorum, beatus Augustinus, tractans
illud Iohannis I°, "Verbum caro factum est, et vidimus gloriam eius."
Et ita hoc correlarium Ihesum valde dehonorat dolosa calliditate,
15 eum universalizans.
Conclusio decima: Deus absque mutatione sui in aequalitate
essendi omnia est in unitate cum humanitate Ihesu maximi.
Patet, quia cum Deus sit supremae aequalitatis et simplicitatis,
tunc Deus, ut est in omnibus, non est secundum gradus in ipsis
20 quasi se gradatim et particulariter communicando. Et cum omnia
sine diversitate graduali esse non possint, tunc omnia sunt in

---

37 21 accipit: accepit *T*   26 punctum: *habet* v   puncta *MT*   33 maximitati:
ex maximitate *corr. M*
38 6 adversus: *add.* v   12 beatus: *om. T*   17 Ihesu: Christi *post* Ihesu *scribit
et del. T*

Deo secundum se cum graduum diversitate. Ergo et maximus
homo Ihesus in ipso Deo non aliter quam maxime esse potest.
Haec nefanda conclusio aequalitatem asserit essendi divinitatis
25 et humanitatis; pariter et Deum non simplicem sed compositum
affirmat, ob diversitatem graduum omnium in eo gradualiter
distincte existentium.
Correlarium primum: Christi humanitas, cum sit maxima,
sic totam speciei potentiam amplectitur ut sit cuiuslibet hominis
30 talis essendi aequalitas quod ei specialissime coniuncta et Christus
sit ipse idem homo unione perfectissima, cuiuslibet numero salvo.
Patet, quia hoc agit maximitas humanae naturae ut quidquid
Ihesus sua passione meruit, illi meruerunt qui unum sunt cum
ipso, salva differentia graduum meriti secundum differentiam gra-
35 duum unionis cuiusque cum ipso per fidem caritate formatam.
39 Quanta venenositas huius correlarii! quia tollit singularitatem
humanitatis Christi, videlicet quod Christus non fuerit singularis
homo sed universalis. Cuius humanitatem dicit Deum non per
unionem hypostaticam sed per abstractissimam intelligentiam,
5 ponens essentiam Christi essentiam cuiuslibet hominis. Ex hoc
quia species humana tota, ponit etiam Christum quemlibet hominem,
et sic quilibet homo esset Christus. Et quod periculosissimum
est, meritum Christi ascribit maximitati humanae naturae, non
Christo gratuite nos iustificante, inimicus gratiae, quantum in se
10 esset suffocans Christi iustitiam, non valens dicere cum propheta:
"Quoniam non cognovi litteraturam, introibo in potentias Domini;
memorabor iustitiae tuae solius." Nihil enim ascribit de merito
iustitiae Christi, unde omne nostrum meritum. Et ulterius ait nos
meruisse quod Christus meruit; et tunc adiungens de caritate, ut
15 suae nequitiae per fidei quemdam superducat apparentem colorem
religionis. Longe enim differunt ab invicem unio specifica humanae
naturae, unio hypostatica humanae naturae cum divina in Christo,
et unio affectualis sive caritativa mentis cum Deo, de qua apostolus
I^a Corintheorum VI°: "Qui adhaeret Domino, unus spiritus est."
20 Quam differentiam unionum ignorans hic scriba doctae ignorantiae
et nihil probat, et sic nedum rerum naturalium sed etiam gra-

38 34 differentia: differentia *(sed confuse scriptum)* habet *T*   35 formatam: habet *v*   formata *M*   firmata *T*
39 1 venenositas: venositas *M*   5 cuiuslibet: cuilibet *M*   7 periculosissimum: periculosum *T*   9 gratuite: *ex* gratuitate *corr. M*   iustificante: iustificanti *T*
16 religionis: *habet M, sed non perfecte scriptum est*

De Ignota Litteratura

tialium ordinem sic impie confundit, naturam ignorans et gratiam abiens in consilium impiorum.

Correlarium secundum: Humanitas Ihesu ut unita divinitati
25 plurimum absoluta est. Patet, quia secundum hoc fuit absoluta a tempore et supra tempus et incorruptibilis simpliciter, et veritas corporis temporaliter contracta, quasi signum, imago, et umbra veritatis corporalis supertemporalis. Qua per mortem sublata, remansit in resurrectione Ihesus in corpore supertemporali. Cuius
30 et humanitas sursum fuit in incorruptibilitate divina radicata inseparabiliter.

Correlarium hoc in se est omnino pestiferum, quia interimit veram Christi humanitatem. Si namque homo Christus secundum humanitatem ex anima et humana carne, ut dicit symbolum
35 Athanasii, quomodo humanitas Christi est plurima absoluta? Nec
40 stat probatio, quia assumpta a Verbo Christi humanitas non fuit absoluta a tempore, quia cum venit plenitudo temporis, teste apostolo, missus est Christus. Ergo eius humanitas non fuit absoluta a tempore nec super tempus et incorruptibilis simpliciter, quia
5 tunc non fuisset Christus vere mortuus. Insuper in huiusmodi probatione negat veritatem corporis Christi ac eiusdem resurrectionem, universalizatione humanitatis Christi, quam abstractio suae intelligentiae sibi fallaciter suggerebat, privans nos sic Christi gratuitis beneficiis in sua temporali humanitate nobis benignissime
10 exhibitis.

Correlarium tertium: Eadem est humanitas Christi et omnium hominum, distinctione numerali individuorum inconfusa remanente. Patet, cum non sit nisi una indivisibilis humanitas quae est omnium hominum specifica essentia. Quapropter omnium hominum qui
15 temporaliter ante aut post Christum fuerunt aut erunt humanitas in Christo immortalitatem induisse, ut etiam post resurrectionem perpetuo sint incorruptibiles.

Mirabile correlarium! cuius prima pars omnes homines singulariter identificat, insinuans universale reale identitate mul-
20 tiplicatum, quod est erroneum, cum soli naturae divinae conveniat in identitate naturae se multiplicare suppositaliter sive personaliter. Secunda autem pars eiusdem correlarii contradicit primae, videlicet quod eadem et distincta numeraliter inconfuse sit Christi et omnium hominum humanitas.
25 Correlarium quartum: Quilibet beatorum, servata veritate

39 22 impie: *ex* impii *corr. M*   24 Ihesu: *bis T* (Ihesu[1] *del. T*)
40 19 identitate: ydemptitate (=identitate) *non proprie abbreviat M*   22 primae: quod *post* prime *scribit et del. T*   23 numeraliter: numeratur *M*

sui proprii esse, est in Christo Ihesu Christus, et per ipsum in
Deo Deus. Patet, nam ecclesia unitatem plurium salva cuiusque
personali veritate dicit absque confusione naturarum et graduum.
Et unio ecclesiastica coincidit sursum cum unione hypostatica
30 naturarum in Christo, quae ulterius coincidit cum unione absoluta,
quae est Deus. Christus enim est fides et caritas; et in fide
eius omnis vera fides, et in caritate eius omnis caritas vera inclu-
ditur, gradibus tamen distinctis semper remanentibus.
    Correlarium hoc ponit quemlibet beatum Christum et Deum,
35 et fidem et caritatem esse Christum. Insuper discernendo gradua-
41 liter diversas res, continue easdem confundit, et sic discernendo
confundit sicuti ad doctum ignorantem pertinet, ipseque se fatetur
penitus ignorans uniones rerum distinctas et de ecclesia exorbi-
tantissime loquens, et virtutes, fidem scilicet et caritatem, quae
5 sunt accidentia de prima specie qualitatis, substantificans in
Christi naturam.
    Nescio an diebus meis unicum scribam sicut hunc umquam
viderim tam perniciosum, in materia divinitatis et trinitatis personarum, in materia universitatis rerum, in materia Incarnationis
10 Christi, in materia virtutum theologicalium, in materia ecclesiae.
Qui tamen dicit se ex hac docta ignorantia desideriis altius
inflammatum, fortassis loquens de inflammatione a Iehenna
indomabilis linguae non refrenatae et vanae religionis, de qua Iacobi III°.
Quem vos, venerabilis pater, omni conatu fugite, ne sensus vestri
15 ab hoc pseudoapostolo ac operario subdolo se in apostolum
Christi transfigurante, veluti ab astuto serpente seducti corrum-
pantur et excidant a virginitate fidei et simplicitate, quae est in
Christo Ihesu Domino nostro, ad cuius honorem et gloriam hanc
Ignotam Litteraturam vestrae religiositati devotae sic statui conscribere,
20 qui cum Deo Patre et Spiritu Sancto vivit in saecula benedictus.
Amen.

ET SIC EST FINIS SCRIPTIS
CURSORIE HEYDELBERG.

40 28 naturarum: in Christo *post* naturarum *scribit et del.* T   31 est[2]: *om.* T
41 5 substantificans: substanficans *M*   10 theologicalium: theoloycalium *T*
13 linguae: ligue *M* ligwe *T*   19 Litteraturam: Litteratoriam *M*   22-23 ET . . .
HEYDELBERG: *om. M*

INDEX OF PROPER NAMES

Agnes, Princess of Hungary, 83n56
Albert, King of Hungary, 83n56
Algazel, 50-52
Almericus, 61
Ambrose (St.), 56, 65
Anselm, of Canterbury, 89n17
Apuleius, 47
Aquinas, Thomas, 53
Aristotle, 23, 29, 30, 35, 37, 46
Asclepius, 46
Athanasius, 58
Augustine (St.), 38, 50-52, 58, 59, 63
Avicenna, 48, 49, 56
Bede, Pseudo-, 91n64
Boethius, Anicius, 58, 82n19
David, of Dinant, 61
David, the Psalmist, 5, 24, 25, 36
Dionysius, Pseudo-, 3, 46, 47, 49-56, 58, 61, 63, 65
Duclow, Donald, 78n28
Eckhart, Meister, 3, 17, 18, 26, 27, 31, 57-59
Elsbeth, Queen of Hungary, 83n56
Elymas, 46
Erigena, John Scotus, 56, 61
Eugene, IV (Pope), 3
Fuehrer, Mark, 78n28
Fulgentius, 65
Gaius, 50
Guldenschaf, John, 58
Haubst, Rudolf, 3, 4, 6, 15, 76n5
Henry, of Mechlin, 52
Herennius, 65
Heron, Germain, 78n28
Hierotheus, 65
Hoffmann, Ernst, 14
Hugh, of St. Victor, 56
Isaac, the Patriarch, 44
Isaiah, the Prophet, 24
Jerome (St.), 52
Jesus, *passim*
John Andrea, see 'Vigevius, John'
John, the Apostle, 37, 65

John, the Baptist, 51
John, Bishop of Strasburg, 26
John, of Gelnhausen (Abbot of Maulbronn), 3, 21, 45, 82n2, 89n5
John, of Mossbach, 61
Klibansky, Raymond, 14, 16, 77n12, 90n29,n42, 91n46, 92n80,n81,n85, 93n122
Koch, Josef, 17
Leo (Pope), 65
Maimonides, Moses, 86n125
Martin, Vincent, 7-13, 79n31,n35, 80n55
Mary, the Virgin, 26
Maulbronn, Abbot of, see 'John, of Gelnhausen'
Maximus, the Confessor, 56, 91n64
Moses, 30, 33, 55, 56, 59
Nicholas, of Cusa, *passim*
Nicholas (Pope), 49
Parmenides, 34, 63
Paul (St.), 'Teacher of the Gentiles,' 5, 31, 46, 49, 51, 58, 60, 62, 65, 79n31
Plato, 47, 49, 62, 78n28
Philo, Judaeus, 44, 47, 52
Porphyry, 28
Proclus, 62
Ritter, Gerhard, 3, 5, 6
Robert, of Lincoln, 56
Socrates, 31, 36, 43, 44, 47, 62, 78n28
Spinoza, Baruch, 79n28
Steer, Georg, 4
Theodorus, 61
Thomas (St.), see 'Aquinas, Thomas'
Timothy, 46, 56
Traversari, Ambrose, 49, 89n10, 91n55
Trismegistus, Hermes, 26, 46
Vansteenberghe, Edmond, 4, 5, 14, 15, 77n10,n12
Vercelli, Abbot of, see 'Gallus, Thomas'
Victorinus, Marius, 61
Vigevius, John, 61
Wenck, John, *passim*

119